Lessons from
My Ordinary Life

Loretta Swan

ISBN 978-1-63874-589-1 (paperback)
ISBN 978-1-63874-590-7 (digital)

Copyright © 2021 by Loretta Swan

All rights reserved. No part of this publication may be reproduced, distributed, or transmitted in any form or by any means, including photocopying, recording, or other electronic or mechanical methods without the prior written permission of the publisher. For permission requests, solicit the publisher via the address below.

Christian Faith Publishing, Inc.
832 Park Avenue
Meadville, PA 16335
www.christianfaithpublishing.com

Scriptures in this book have been quoted from the following versions of the Bible:

Scripture quotations from (MSG). The Message Bible. Copyright by Eugene H. Peterson 1993, 1994, 1995, 1996, 2000, 2001, 2002.

Scripture quotations from **(NIV) HOLY BIBLE, NEW INTERNATIONAL VERSION®, Copyright 1973, 1978, 1984, 2011 by Biblica, Inc.®**

Scripture quotations from (KJV) The Authorized King James Version. Rights in the Authorized Version in the United Kingdom are vested in the Crown. Reproduced by permission of the Crown's patented, Cambridge University Press.

Printed in the United States of America

Contents

Introduction 7

Section 1 From My Youth 9
   1 My Birth 11
   2 The Prayer of Faith 13
   3 The Words of My Mouth 15
   4 Bullies on the Bus 19
   5 Temptation 22
   6 Find a Need and Fill It 24
   7 Showing the Christian Spirit 26

Section 2 My Children/Grandchildren 29
   1 My Daughter's Shoes 31
   2 Laying a Foundation 33
   3 Teaching Trust 36
   4 Apprehension 38
   5 Gifts 40
   6 The Faith of a Child 44

Section 3 As a Young Mother 49
   1 Living in Church Community 51
   2 The Ugly Duckling 55
   3 Higher than I Can Reach 58
   4 Finding God's Calling 60

5   Little Is Much, Extravagant Giving.....................63
  6   Affirmations..66
  7   Sharing the Reason for Hope.........................71
  8   Vacations and Smiles 74

Section 4 Adult Children 77
  1   Give Them a Way Out 79
  2   Acknowledging God......................................82
  3   The Christmas Tree 86
  4   The Gift of Time...89
  5   Seeing God...92
  6   What Do These Stones Mean?......................95

Section 5 Endings or Beginnings.......................................99
  1   Heartbreak 101
  2   The Opposite of Love 104
  3   Not a Waste!...106
  4   Lost Identity...108
  5   Forgiveness...110
  6   God's Provisions...114
  7   Deciding to Go to School at Fifty-Five.............117
  8   Closing the Door on the Past 119
  9   The Kids 121

Section 6 Africa...123
  1   Like That Will Ever Happen! 125
  2   Opposition..127
  3   Katie's Missing Suitcase 129
  4   Emmanuel's Story.......................................131
  5   Finding Goats 134
  6   The Flight Home 138

Section 7 Moving Forward with a Push 141
  1 Some Things Are Worth Fighting For 143
  2 Buying My Trailer 145
  3 The Fall I Will Never Forget 148
  4 Helping Hands 150
  5 Sowing Seeds in the Midst of Drought 152
  6 Running Out of Money to Finish School 154
  7 Provisions to Finish School 156
  8 My Yearly Word 158
  9 Saying Yes to God's Will 161
10 The Case of Full Disclosure 164
11 Can You Hear Me Now? 166
12 Miracles 168
13 Ode to Joy 171

Introduction

My purpose in writing my life experiences is to show how God has been faithful and my strength through all my years and to help other women in their walk with God. I also wanted to help my seven granddaughters learn from my mistakes and find strength in God's faithfulness.

In Romans 12:1–2 (MSG), the apostle Paul admonishes believers: "So here's what I want you to do, God helping you: Take your everyday, ordinary life—your sleeping, eating, going to work, and walking around life—and place it before God as an offering. Embracing what God does for you is the best thing you can do for him. Do not become so well-adjusted to your culture that you fit into it without even thinking. Instead, fix your attention on God. You will be changed from the inside out. Readily recognize what He wants from you and quickly respond to it. Unlike the culture around you, always dragging you down to its level of immaturity, God brings the best out of you, develops well-formed maturity in you." That is what this book is all about, God changing me from the inside out through my every day, ordinary life as I responded to what He wanted me to do. As you read how God has helped me, I hope you will find encouragement and strength.

Section 1
From My Youth

Chapter 1

My Birth

My mother went to the hospital in labor before she was full-term with me. The nurse tried to send her home, but Mom said, "This is my fourth delivery, and I am telling you, I am going to have this baby tonight!" The nurse put my mother in a room, did not check her (this was before ultrasounds) and forgot about her. Several hours later, Mom screamed, and the nurse came running in the room just in time to catch me. I was all of five pounds, five ounces. This was back when five-pound babies did not survive. Now, the medical field is saving babies who weigh less than one pound. Amazing! I also had yellow jaundice, the nurses placed my incubator next to the window during the daytime, I was in an incubator for over a month until I weighed seven pounds, five ounces. Then my parents could take me home.

There were no car seats back in the fifties either. So Dad had one of his shoeboxes in the car, and that was how I traveled home, in a shoebox on my brother's lap.

MY BIRTH

I did not keep milk down and lost weight the first few days I was home. The doctor told my mother to switch me to goats' milk, and I started gaining weight.

> From birth, I have relied on you; you brought me forth from my mother's womb. I will ever praise you. (Psalm 71:6 NIV)

> I praise you because I am fearfully and wonderfully made; your works are wonderful; I know that full well. (Psalm 139:14 NIV)

What I learned from my mother is that (1) I was a miracle, but I think all babies are; (2) if doctors or nurses make assumptions without checking, trust your instincts and stand your ground, insist they run the tests.

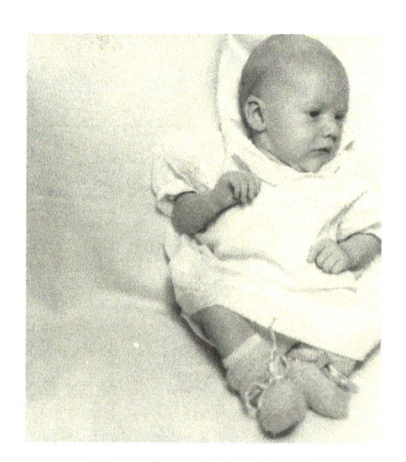

October 21st 1953
4 weeks old

Chapter 2

The Prayer of Faith

I was about seven years old; I had been sick for several days and was running a high fever. We did not have medical insurance, so there was no being taken to the doctor. My mom stayed home from church with me that Sunday. The pastor's wife knew the only way my mom would stay home from church was if there was a problem, and with my dad not having given his heart to Christ yet and being an alcoholic, she was concerned. So she came over to check on us. I do not remember much, but I do remember her sitting on the side of my bed, taking my hands in hers, and praying for God to heal me. She left, and I fell asleep. When I woke up the next morning, the fever was gone. I sat up and wanted something to eat. The next day, I felt well enough to return to school. This was the first of many healings God would do.

What I learned, If God brings someone to my mind, I go see them, pray for them, or call them, or send them a card or a text, letting them know I have prayed for them. If I or a family member is sick, this verse says for us to call the elders and ask for prayer:

THE PRAYER OF FAITH

Is any sick among you? Let him call for the elders of the church, and let them pray over him, anointing him with oil in the name of the Lord: And the prayer of faith shall save the sick, and the Lord shall raise him up. (James 5:14–15a KJV)

Chapter 3

The Words of My Mouth

I could write a set of books on what I have learned and am still learning when it comes to what I say or when I say it. Proverbs 25:11 (NIV) says, "A word aptly spoken is like apples of gold in settings of silver." In other words, they bring beauty to the soul. Too many times, I have spoken words at the wrong time or in the wrong place; and instead of creating beauty, they were hurtful and anything but lovely.

I was around eight years old, the middle child of five, and the oldest girl. Trying to get attention from my parents was no easy task as mom was a rescuer. It did not matter if she rescued children or dogs. She could not stand to see anyone hurting or doing without. We always had a full house. My mother was a foster mother before there was a foster program. She also worked full-time, so there was even less time to divvy up. Back then, my eight-year-old mind thought the best way to get attention was to talk, *a lot*! I thought that made me look smarter; unfortunately, I became a nuisance instead!

I remember one Sunday, about five years later, we were at church when the pastor read this verse from Proverbs 17:28 (NIV), "Even a fool is thought wise if he keeps silent and discerning if he holds his tongue." The light came on in my head. *I have this backward. I just need to shut up and people will think I am smart.* It was no easy task as a thirteen-year-old to change my behavior. I memorized and prayed Psalms 141:3 (NIV), which says, "Set a guard over my mouth, O Lord; keep watch over the door of my lips". I also started praying Psalms 19:14 (KJV): "Let the words of my mouth and the meditation of my heart be acceptable in thy sight, O Lord, my strength and my redeemer." The Holy Spirit would bring these verses to my mind when I embarked on yet another episode of running off at the mouth. This was the beginning of many lessons on the power of my spoken word.

During high school, my friend and I decided to try an experiment. We did not have any classes together, but there was a girl—let's call her Susie—that was in my first period class, my friend's second period class, my third period class, and so on, for the remainder of the day. The experiment went like this: When I saw Susie in first period, I asked her if she was feeling well. She said she was and wondered why I had asked. I told her she did not look well (sad to admit it was a lie). My friend asked her the same question during second period. This time Susie said she was starting to feel ill. She asked my friend why and was told she did not look well. Third period, Susie was not in class, nor fourth, fifth, or sixth period. The next day, Susie was back in class. When I saw her, I asked her what happened; she replied she went home sick. I felt wretched for planting that thought in her head.

That experiment taught me a powerful lesson. A few weeks afterward, I came across this verse from Ephesians 4:29 (KJV): "Let no corrupt communication proceed out of your mouth but that which is good to the use of edifying that it may minister grace unto the hearers." From that day forward, I decided to work at edifying other people with the words of my mouth, ministering grace (*un*deserved favor) to the hearer. Shortly afterward, I heard a pastor preach about Barnabas from Acts 4:36 (NIV). He said the name Barnabas meant "son of encouragement." Later I asked the Lord to make me a "daughter of encouragement."

I have worked on becoming a "daughter of encouragement" ever since. Ministering grace to others is a lifelong learning process. I thought I was doing well until my brother died in 2007. Christian friends came to "comfort" me, saying things like, "He is in a better place now," or "God would not want you to cry but rejoice as he is in heaven and no longer in pain." Those words did not comfort me; they made me angry. I was grieving. A few days later, I realized I too had fallen into that trap of quoting clichés and had been a "miserable comforter." I asked God to forgive me and help me. Shortly after my brother's passing, I came across Romans 12:15 (KJV): "Rejoice with them that do rejoice, and weep with them that weep." I began to practice that verse. I realized how important it was to just hold someone in your arms without words, to cry with them, to be there for them, and to let them tell their story. This is what brings healing. Not just saying, "If you need anything call me." It is better to show up and sit with them, to cry with them and let them share their heart with you. That truly comforts and ministers grace to people during their saddest time. Jesus was our example, He wept at the tomb of Lazarus.

What I learned: I have learned (1) the importance of being there for others in their grieving and in their celebrating; (2) taking a deep breath before speaking, this gives me time to allow the Holy Spirit to guard my lips; (3) how powerful what we say is, it can easily encourage or discourage others.

Chapter 4

Bullies on the Bus

In my family growing up, we were never allowed to fight—at home, with each other, or at school. If we did fight, we were punished in a way that made it not worth fighting. My sister and I were in junior high, and word must have gotten around because two girls who disembarked from the school bus at the same stop as my sister and I started tripping us as we stepped off the bus. We would end up running home with skinned knees, crying while they called us names.

Our dad worked for the school district and knew the principle. He went to talk with him. The principle told dad that because it did not happen on school property, there was nothing he could do. Dad also knew the bus driver and went to talk with him. He also said that because it did not happen on the bus, there was nothing he could do. He did however confirm our story. Dad gave us permission to fight back but not to use our hand or fist. I was so excited; I spent that evening planning on how to fight back.

The next day, I let my sister step off the bus first, they tripped her. I stepped down, took my three-ring binder, and swung knocking one girl on her butt, then I yelled, "If you ever trip us again, you will get worse than that." She said, "I thought you were not allowed to fight." My reply was, "My dad gave us permission to fight." She ran home crying and never bullied us again. This was a physical battle. I learned there are some things worth fighting for.

We do need to remember, most battles in life are spiritual.

> For we wrestle not against flesh and blood but against principalities, against powers, against the rulers of the darkness of this world, against spiritual wickedness in high places. (Ephesians 6:12 KJV)

> Be alert and of sober mind. Your enemy, the devil, prowls around like a roaring lion, looking for someone to devour. (1 Peter 5:8 NIV)

Jesus declares, "The thief comes only to steal and kill and destroy; I have come that they may have life and have it to the full" (John 10:10 NIV). Paul exhorts us to "fight the good fight of faith" (1 Timothy 6:12 NIV) and to "put on the full armor of God so that you can take your stand against the devil's schemes" (Ephesians 6:11 NIV). All but one piece of the armor is for our protection.

> The weapons we fight with are not the weapons of the world. On the contrary, they have divine power to demolish strongholds. (2 Corinthians 10:4 NIV)

We have an enemy, but our heavenly Father has given us permission to fight him. James admonishes us to "submit yourselves therefore to God. Resist the devil, and he *will flee* from you" (James 4:7 KJV). So how do we resist the devil?—by using the Sword of the Spirit, which is the Word of God. Quote it at him.

What I learned: (1) how powerful our spoken word is—it can bring encouragement or discouragement; (2) if I fight, it gives God the opportunity to give the victory; (3) how powerful speaking the word of God is.

Chapter 5

Temptation

I have been very blessed to have many Sunday school teachers and youth leaders who understood the importance of memorizing scripture. In fifth grade, our children's church leader set up a store with toys and games he purchased and gave each item points. He then gave us a list of Bible verses with point values to memorize. For instance, the Lord's Prayer was worth 500 points; the Beatitudes, worth 500 points; the Fruit of the Spirit, worth 250 points, and the 23rd Psalm was worth 250 points. Each week we would come in to class, and he had a time where we could quote the verse/verses we had memorized. He then kept track of our points. And at the end of each quarter, we went shopping with the points we had earned. This was a fun way to memorize Bible verses.

One of the verses I memorized as a child was Psalms 119:11 (KJV): "Thy word have I hid in mine heart that I might not sin against thee." In my freshman year of high school, I had one friend in school; I shall call her Peggy. We had an agreement. Each day when we got to school, we would give each other our lunch money to hold for the other person until we found something we wanted to buy then ask for it back. It was like a savings account. I walked to school each day. On my way one day, I was tempted to go into a five-and-dime store and use Peggy's money to buy a candy bar. That day I left the house before I had breakfast and before my mom gave me my lunch money. I was walking on the other side of the street from the store. The moment after the temptation, the Holy Spirit brought this verse to my mind: "No temptation has overtaken you except what is common to mankind. And God is faithful; he will not let you be tempted beyond what you can bear. But when you are tempted, he will also provide a way out so that you can endure it" (1 Corinthians 10:13 NIV). And he whispered to my heart, "Stay on this side of the street." I wish I had listened. I went over and bought a twenty-five-cent candy bar and ate it on my way to school. When I arrived, Peggy met me and wanted her money. I gave her what I had left. She had been keeping track and knew there was missing money. She became angry with me with just cause and said she was no longer my friend. I had violated her trust.

What I learned: (1) God always makes a way of escape; (2) it is up to us to listen and obey; (3) violating trusts ruins friendships.

Chapter 6

Find a Need and Fill It

I was an eighth grader in what used to be called junior high, which is now called middle school. I remember hearing from adults that if you wanted to be successful, find a need and fill it. I went to a football game one Friday evening and noticed the other team had cheerleaders, but our team did not. So I decided to create a cheerleading team. The team consisted of myself as the captain, my sister, and six other girls from my homeroom class. There was no money for outfits, so we wore our PE clothes, which were white shorts and a white snap-up blouse. We made our own pompoms out of newspapers and learned a few simple cheers then showed up at the next football game. We had so much fun. I was so proud of my success. Then the next day, I was called into the principal's office. I had never been called in to the principal's office before; I was not sure why. He very kindly started explaining to me there was a proper way to do things. I should have brought my idea to him for approval, then money could have been given for pompoms. He said I had embarrassed the school with the homemade pompoms. He liked that I saw a need, but things would change. A teacher had to be in charge, not me. He had already chosen one, and we were to meet with her after school that day with all the other cheerleaders. We met, and I was publicly demoted. That evening, in my despair, I was reminded of this verse: "Pride goes before destruction, a haughty spirit before a fall" (Proverbs 16:18 NIV).

There was one picture in the yearbook of the cheerleading team. My sister and I were in the back of the line where we could not be seen. I was very thankful that we moved the end of that term.

What I learned: (1) There is a proper way to do things; and (2) even when I am successful not to become proud in my accomplishments, it is God who gives the ideas.

Chapter 7

Showing the Christian Spirit

The organization my parents were pastors through had a program for teenagers called Bible Quizzing. Any church that wanted to participate just needed four teenagers to sign up with a coach. Our team consisted of myself (I was eighteen. Next year would be my last year with the team), my two sisters, and one other girl from the church. Our mother was our coach. Each year a different book of the Bible was chosen to study. Our first year, we studied the book of Romans. The next year was First and Second Corinthians. We started studying in the fall and by spring would compete with other church teams. There were general questions but also specific verses we had to quote word-for-word, no mistakes. The first competition was against other churches in the organization within our state. The first year, we lost the state championship. The second year, there were no other churches competing, so we won by default. We then proceeded to the district competition, which for us meant a trip to southern California from Washington state. We won that one. We then had to go to nationals in Ohio.

We were one of three teams that made it to nationals. We had to raise funds for the trip and food. We slept in churches or rest areas along the way to save money. It unfortunately was not a very pleasant competition because the other team's captains and coaches challenged the judges on every question they did not win. It was an awfully long day. We came in third place with a trophy. As we were walking out the church it was held at, the janitor, who had been there all day cleaning and watching, said to my mom and dad, "Your team won first place."

My dad corrected him and said, "No, we won third place."

The janitor said, "Your team showed the best Christian spirit. In my book, they took first place because they showed respect."

That was the greatest compliment he could have given us. It reminded me of this verse: "But the fruit of the Spirit is love, joy, peace, forbearance, kindness, goodness, faithfulness, gentleness, and self-control. Against such things, there is no law" (Galatians 5:22–23 NIV).

What I learned that day proved to me that no matter how much of the Bible a person knows, if it is not put into action, it is inconsequential.

Section 2

My Children/Grandchildren

Chapter 1

My Daughter's Shoes

My parents had scheduled for a missionary to come to their church to share with the congregation. They needed to be picked up from the airport, but my parents were unable to go pick them up. So we were asked to go to the airport and provide transportation to the church. The flight had been delayed by an hour, so we stayed at the airport and allowed our three-year-old daughter to run around while we waited. A man approached us and said, "Are you aware your daughter is severely bowlegged?" I had not ever noticed. He then said, "She needs to be in corrective shoes now, or she will be in braces by the time she starts school." I informed him we did not have insurance. He reached in his pocket and pulled out a business card. He wrote a phone number on the back and said, "If you will call this number, I will pay for her shoes." What a gracious gift! That Monday, I called and made the appointment. Upon arrival at the office, I gave the doctor the other man's business card and told him the story. My daughter's shoes were made. She wore them for a whole year. I still have them in her keepsake box to remind her and myself that God provided for her even when we did not know there was a need. She now stands tall and is so beautiful. This taught me a great lesson to always look for ways to bless others.

A friend, years later, said to me, "Why is it the people who have the least are the greatest givers?" I think it is because we have been blessed the most and want to pay it forward. I especially love this verse: "Share with the Lord's people who are in need. Practice hospitality" (Romans 12:13 NIV).

One other thing I learned from the doctor was to have my daughter sit with her legs crossed in front of her and not to sit on her feet behind her. This also taught me to engage in the acts of kindness as often as I am able.

Chapter 2

Laying a Foundation

There was a time when I watched my grown children make choices. I knew was going to cause them grief. When the time came for them to reap what they had sown, my heart broke. Did I miss the mark as a mother? Did I not teach them values? As I cried before the Lord, he spoke these words to my heart, "As a parent, you only get to lay a foundation. There comes a time in each child's life when they must build upon that foundation. They may, and most do, start out building with wood, hay, or stubble, stuff that will not stand the storms of life. But when the storms come, and they will, what they have built will be destroyed, but the foundation will remain, and they will have the opportunity to learn from their experience and rebuild."

What is the foundation we get to lay? We are to share with our children (and grandchildren) what God has done for us. In Joshua 4:1–10 is the story about the nation of Israel finally crossing the Jordan River into the Promised Land after wandering for forty years in the desert. God instructed Joshua to select twelve men, one from each tribe of Israel, and instructed them to pick up a stone from the river, place it on their shoulder, and carry it across the Jordan and set them down in the place they camped that night (in the Promised Land). The reason God had instructed them to do this was that it would be a sign that when their children asked what the stones meant, then they could share the story of how God cut off the waters of Jordan, and they passed over safely into the Promised Land. Laying a foundation means telling your children (and grandchildren) when God answers your prayers, provides, and blesses both you and others. As they see and hear what God is doing for you, it will encourage their faith and build a foundation.

In my many years in church, one of the greatest tragedies I have seen are parents who, instead of sharing the great things God has done and is doing, get in the car after church and talk badly about the pastor, staff, or other Christians in front of their children. This will destroy your children's faith! People are human and make mistakes. Keep your children's focus on God, not people.

David, who had killed the giant Goliath, had been anointed by the prophet of God years earlier to be the next king of Israel. Saul, the current king, was also anointed at one time, but he chose to violate God's laws. After conquering Goliath, David was brought into King Saul's palace and placed in charge of his army. After King Saul heard the maidens praising David for his conquests and victories, Saul became jealous. David had to flee for his life, and Saul pursued him for many years. David had a right to the throne of Israel, he had been anointed to be the next king, yet David knew that one day God would give him what God had promised. Once David and his men were hiding in a cave from Saul's army when Saul came into the cave to relieve himself. David's men said, "Now is your chance, kill Saul." David did not slay Saul when an opportunity presented itself. David knew a mighty principle and later wrote it in Psalms 105:15 (NIV): "Do not touch my anointed ones; do my prophets no harm." When you talk badly about those God has placed in authority, you are harming their reputation. But mostly, we destroy our children's foundation and faith.

So what are we to do if we disagree with the pastor, staff, or other Christians? We are to pray the Colossians Prayer for them. Nothing delights a pastor's heart more than to know people are praying for him and being thankful for his words of exhortation. When you get in the car, share with your family a verse or a thought God placed in your heart during the sermon. Keep your focus on what God is doing for you and others and what God is speaking to your heart. By doing so, you will be laying a great foundation for your children and grandchildren.

What I learned is to be careful of what I say, especially around children as we can easily tear down their foundation and destroy their faith.

Chapter 3

Teaching Trust

During my first marriage, we lived at or below the poverty line during the years our children were growing up. They would often come home from school saying they needed this or that for a class, to which I usually replied, "We don't have the money for that." One afternoon my daughter, Ann, came home with the usual request for something she needed for school, and I gave my usual response. Only this time, God spoke to my heart and asked, "Are you teaching your children to trust me?" He then reminded me of James 4:2b (NIV), which states "You do not have because you do not ask God." Wow, what a thought. I was not asking God for the things my children needed nor trusting God to take care of our needs, and I certainly was not teaching my children to ask or trust God. I asked God for forgiveness then called Ann into the room. I shared with her what God had spoken to my heart. We said a prayer together, asking God to meet the need. Within the week, someone slipped a one-hundred-dollar bill into the mail slot of our front door. I quickly ran out to see who it was, but there was no one around. I believe it was an angel or at least a person that was sent by God to bless us. That money not only paid for what Ann needed for school but also took care of another bill.

This experience encouraged me to put James 4:2 into practice and start asking God for what we needed so my children would see Him as the loving heavenly Father he is who takes care of our needs.

Teaching my children trust in God and trusting Him myself has not been an easy road. It is not easy because we live in a world where trust is easily broken.

What I have come to realize is the joy and peace that comes from trusting God. Romans 15:13 (NIV) best describes it: "May the God of hope fill you with all joy and peace as you trust in Him so that you may overflow with hope by the power of the Holy Spirit."

Chapter 4

Apprehension

My daughter, Ann, had a good friend, Kim. They had been friends since elementary school. Either Kim was at our house or Ann was at her house. Ann had gone camping with her family several times. And they often baked cookies or made meals together at our house.

They were now in high school. Kim had called and ask if she could pick up Ann to go with her to the mall on Saturday. I said yes. Kim arrived Saturday to pick Ann up, she came in the house. Ann put on her coat and started out the door. At which time, I adamantly told Ann she could not go. Ann said "Mom, my chores are done. You said I could go! What am I being punished for?" I had no answers for her, just a strong apprehension. After several minutes of standing my ground, Ann took off her coat and told Kim to go without her, but she was mad. She went to her room and stayed there till dinner. After dinner, Kim called and told Ann she had been in a car accident on her way to the mall. She had been T-boned right where Ann would have been sitting. Kim told her, had she gone, she probably would have died in the accident. I then realized it was the Spirit that had given me the apprehension. Romans 8:6b (NIV) says, "The mind governed by the Spirit is life and peace." I wish I could say I listen to the Spirit like that all the time, but that has not been the case. Many times I have chosen to not listen and have had to deal with the consequences.

What I learned is how important it is to listen to the Holy Spirit. My life would have had less stress and more peace.

Chapter 5

Gifts

Nicole and Marie, two of my eleven grandchildren, were about ten and nine years old when we went for a drive. God had been encouraging me to help my grandchildren find their gifts, therefore I shared with them the story in Matthew 25:15–23 where a man gave to his servants what the scripture calls "talents," which was money, however the principles remain true pertaining to gifts as well.

> "To one he gave five talents of money, to another two talents, and to another one talent, each according to his ability. Then he went on his journey. The man who had received the five talents went at once and put his money to work and gained five more. So also, the one with the two talents gained two more. After a long time, the master of those servants returned and settled accounts with them. The man who had received the five talents brought the other five. "Master," he said, "you

entrusted me with five talents. See, I have gained five more." The master replied, "Well done, good and faithful servant! You have been faithful with a few things. I will put you in charge of many things. Come and share your master's happiness!" The man with the two talents also came. "Master," he said, "you entrusted me with two talents. See, I have gained two more." His master replied, "Well done, good and faithful servant! You have been faithful with a few things. I will put you in charge of many things. Come and share your master's happiness!"

As I shared with the girls that God has also given to each person gifts just as 1 Corinthians 7:7b (NIV) states, "But each man has his own gift from God; one has this gift, another has that," and that God's desire is for them to discover that gift, and as 2 Timothy 1:6 (NIV) says, to "fan into flame the gift of God, which is in you." As we discussed the story of the "talents," I shared what some talents might be. For example, someone who was good working with computers, they liked to take them apart and try to put them back together—that is a gift. But they need to make that gift grow.

"How could they do that?" I asked—by going to school and gaining an education in computer repairs. Or say, someone loved playing a musical instrument. How could they make that gift grow?—by taking music lessons.

Nicole became extremely excited and said she knew what gift God had given her. I asked her to share with us what she thought that was. She exuberantly shouted out, "Singing!" And she was right! I also mentioned she had a love for cooking, and that too was a gift. I asked her how she could make her gift of singing grow. After a few moments of thought, she said she would join the choir at school. Which she did, all during middle school and into high school. She is now part of the worship team at her church. As far as cooking, I bought her an apron and her first cookbook for Christmas that year. And for the next three years, I bought her more cookbooks. She is now in college, working toward a degree to become a nutritionist, helping people learn to eat healthier.

On that trip, Marie could not think of a gift she had. So I promised I would pray with her that God would reveal what her gift was. That very next day, she came home from school so excited about a star she received on a story she had written. Remember, she was only nine years old. She called me up and asked if she could read it to me. Of course I said yes. After she read the story, I exclaimed, "Marie, I know what your gift is!" But before I could finish my sentence, she yelled, "Writing!" We discussed how she could make her gift grow. A writer uses words to tell the story, so she would need to increase her vocabulary. She would need paper and pencils to keep writing. For Christmas, you guessed it, I bought her a dictionary, a thesaurus, some special pencils, and writing paper. Today Marie is in college, working on her degree to teach kindergarten and write children's books.

Recently we discovered Marie also has an artistic talent. She discovered this her senior year at high school. Last week she showed us some sketches and paintings she had done. We decided to invest in her art talent and order her a professional adult art kit. We allowed her to pick it out. It should arrive this week. I mentioned to her today, maybe she will do the illustrations in her own books.

What I learned is to help children find their gifts and then invest in them.

Chapter 6

The Faith of a Child

I remember the day well; it was a hot Sunday afternoon in August. After church, we had been invited to a friend's celebration for his seventy-fifth birthday. We had just purchased our first cell phones the day before and given family our numbers.

My phone rang. It was my sister. She was our parent's full-time caregiver. She informed me that Dad had a heart attack and a stroke. The doctors told her to call the family. They did not think he was going to make it through the night. Richard (my first husband) and I hopped in the car and started the two-and-a-half-hour drive north. We did not go home to get anything.

When we arrived at the hospital, he was in ICU. I went in. He was nonresponsive. I went back out to the waiting room and cried. After I gained my composure, I called my kids to let them know how their grandpa was. I mentioned to my son that he should bring his family to say their goodbyes. One of the nurses heard me talking, she had compassion on me and handed me a book to read called *Tear Soup: A Recipe for Healing After Loss* by Chuck

DeKlyen and Pat Schwiebert. It talks about how everybody grieves differently. It was an extremely helpful book for me.

The next morning, my son arrived with his wife and two girls. His wife had just lost her dad the previous month, so this was very triggering for her and the girls. Nicole, who was eight years old at the time, wanted to go in and see Papa. Her mom and I both felt like it was not a good idea as he was connected to tubes everywhere, but Nicole said, "You didn't let me see my other grandpa, and he died. I want to see Papa." So we changed our minds and decided to go in with her. We asked the nurse, and she approved. We took Nicole by the hand and walked her into the room. She walked up to Papa, put her hand on Papa's hand, and said, "Papa, I don't want you to die, okay?" He sat up in bed. Bells and buzzers went off. Nurses came running in and ushered us out, asking, "What happened?" We told them.

The next day, Papa was still with us and said he was hungry. They brought him in a soft food meal, and he tried feeding himself. He was shaky with his right hand but would not allow us to feed him. He did manage to get some food in his mouth. Later that afternoon, he wanted to get up and use the restroom. The nurse helped him stand up and helped him with a walker to the restroom and back into bed.

The next morning, he did better with breakfast. As he was eating, the family social worker came and sat at the nurse's station. With patients who had a stroke, she helped the family with getting the patient into a rehab center. As she was flipping through Dad's chart, she asked another nurse where they had moved my dad to. The other nurse

THE FAITH OF A CHILD

said he was in the room the social worker was staring into. My dad was doing so well she could not believe it was him.

The next day, they moved Dad out of ICU and into a regular room, three days after they admitted him. Because we had not gone home before we left, we did not have a change of clothes with us nor money to get some. Fortunately, my sister and I wore the same size, so I had some clean things to wear to the hospital each day, and we were able to stay with her at their place to take showers and do some laundry. In the same town as the hospital was in, there was a church in the same organization that our church was part of. I called my pastor and asked what he thought about us contacting them for help with money to purchase Richard some clean clothes. He thought that was a good idea. He even called them to let them know we would be coming. When we arrived, they had a very generous check for us from their benevolence fund. What a blessing! We went to a discount store, and we purchased Richard a couple of outfits. We stayed at the hospital for a couple more days until they decided to send my dad home.

I was reminded of Psalms 8:2a (KJV): "Out of the mouth of babes and sucklings hast thou ordained strength."

> "Yes," replied Jesus, "have you never read from the lips of children and infants, you, Lord, have called forth your praise." (Matthew 21:16b NIV)

Nicole is the one who wanted to go see Papa, and she is the one who spoke to him. God wrought a miracle through a child.

What I learned: (1) Do not discount what God might instill in the heart of our children/grandchildren. He can and often does use them. 2) From that point forward, I kept a packed suitcase in the trunk of the car. So we were never in that predicament again. (3) It is okay to ask for help when needed.

Section 3

As a Young Mother

Chapter 1

Living in Church Community

I was raised in church and have been involved in churches for over fifty years. I was eight years old when I invited Christ into my life. One thing I can tell you is that church is full of imperfect, broken people. You cannot be part of a community of believers long before someone will say or do something to offend you, or you will say or do something to offend someone else. There is no such thing as a perfect church. We are all broken, hurting people. And hurting people, just like hurting dogs, bite. There will come a time you will get your feelings hurt—guaranteed!

One of my personal stories of being hurt in church was when we were attending a small church where a young pastor had just taken over; it was his first church. I played the piano there. While the pastor led song service, he would stare at me in the middle of a song. This went on for several months. I did not know why or what he wanted, so I would shrug my shoulders and continue playing. Years earlier, I played the piano in my parent's church they pastored. (They took churches that were closed and reopened them.) This young pastor knew I had worked with my parents.

After several months, the pastor went to another member of the congregation and told her I was trying to run the church service from the piano. Being the wise woman she was, she told the pastor she was sure that was not the case. He voiced his concern to her that I knew more about running a church than he did. She suggested he meet with me to discuss his concerns. When he talked to me, I was hurt he would even think that. Years later, I realized his inexperience and his knowledge of my experience made him feel insecure. We were able to talk things out, but I was deeply offended and harbored hard feelings against him for some time. I wanted to leave the church, but God did not release us. When I confided in a friend outside the church, she told me "not to be so easily offended." I retorted, "I was not *easily offended!*" And I left my friend's house.

As I drove home, I decided to search the Scriptures to prove I was justified in being offended. As soon as I got home, I pulled out my Bible, my concordance, and started looking up scriptures. Psalms 119:165 (KJV) was the first verse I came across. It reads, "Great peace have they which love thy law: and *nothing* shall offend them." That made me angry. I had a right to be offended. I was falsely accused. Then I read Luke 6:28 (NIV), which says "Pray for those who mistreat you." I wanted to pray like David in Psalms 35:8 (NIV): "May ruin overtake them by surprise. May they fall into the pit to their ruin." Deep inside I knew that is not the kind of prayer God desired me to pray; that is more of a curse than a prayer. Paul gives us an outline of how we are to pray for other believers in Colossians 1:8–11:

1. We are to ask God to fill them with the knowledge of his will through all spiritual wisdom and understanding.
2. We are to pray that they may live a life worthy of the Lord and may please him in every way.
3. We are to pray that they may bear fruit in every good work.
4. We are to pray that they may grow in the knowledge of God.
5. We are to pray that they may be strengthened with all power according to his glorious might.
6. We are to pray that they may have great endurance and patience.
7. And joyfully give thanks to the Father for them. (MSG)

Unfortunately, I was not ready to start praying like that. Then the Lord, who is so gracious, whispered to my heart and said, "If you do not forgive him, he will stand between you and me." That day I made a commitment never to allow anyone to stand between God and myself; that would mean they were closer to God than I was! It was time to forgive him. That is how we are told to pray in the Lord's Prayer. "Forgive us our debts as we also have forgiven our debtors" (Matthew 6:12 NIV). It did not matter whether he asked for forgiveness or not, I knew harboring unforgiveness in my heart would keep me from God. John 20:23 (MSG) declares, "If you forgive someone's sins, they are gone for good. If you do not forgive sins, what are you going to do with them?" I recently heard that harboring unforgiveness is like drinking poison and expecting the other person to die. I knew I had to forgive him. I knelt before the Lord and asked God to forgive me as I forgave the pastor. Such a sweet peace came over my soul; I was ready to start praying the Colossian prayer for him.

Can you imagine how our churches and lives would change for the better if we all prayed the Colossian prayer for each other and practiced true forgiveness? On a personal note, as a believer, can you imagine how much sooner I would have experienced God's joy and peace had I been more willing to forgive him and ask God to forgive me?

What I learned: (1) not to allow anyone to stand between God and myself by harboring unforgiveness and 2) to pray for those I disagree with.

Chapter 2

The Ugly Duckling

My mother worked outside the home. She was the head/training waitress at SkyWay Cafe outside the Los Angeles airport. She worked the breakfast and lunch shifts so she could be home before we arrived home from school. However she left in the morning before we, three girls, woke up. It was our two older brother's responsibility to see us girls eat breakfast and get dressed for school. They were not good about brushing our hair or matching our clothes, so I looked disheveled in most of my school pictures. All the way through middle school, I was the tallest child in my class, which made me very self-conscious. When I reached high school, the boys started to outgrow me. Add to that my "runaway" mouth, which caused my brothers to call me stupid and other names I will not repeat. As a result, you have a girl with a horrid self-image problem and no self-worth. Predictably, I married the first man who said I was beautiful. I did not realize it at the time, but self-worth comes from who God says I am, not from who or what other people say.

THE UGLY DUCKLING

I was married to Richard for five years when my pastor asked me to teach the first- and second-grade Sunday school class. I firmly said *no*. He encouraged me to pray about it and ask God what *he* wanted me to do. I did not ask God. But while in prayer, God would prompt my heart with "I want you to teach that Sunday school class," to which I firmly replied, "*No.*" God and I had this conversation back and forth for several months. I am so thankful God is merciful! One day while I was praying, God prompted my heart again, but this time, I said, "I cannot."

Then God whispered, "Why not?"

I started giving what I call the "Moses's list of excuses" from Exodus chapter 3. Moses started with "who am I that I should?" "What if?" "Oh, Lord, I have never been…" My objections were remarkably similar.

I said "Lord, I am not pretty. What if I am in the store, and one of the kids sees me and points me out to their mother. I would want to run and hide. Who am I to teach others? I am not smart. I never went to college or Bible school."

Then the Lord asked me, "So you see yourself as the ugly duckling, don't you?"

That was exactly how I felt.

Then I heard, "If you will obey me and do the things I ask you to do, I will create in you that beautiful, graceful swan you desire to be."

How could I turn down a proposition like that! Of course, I said yes and started teaching that class. From the moment I said yes to God and my pastor's request, I started collecting ceramic swans as a reminder of what God has done and is still doing in my life.

I am so thankful for his grace and mercy with me throughout my life. I have now taught Sunday school for over twenty-five years. These kids have taught me so much. And I have seen "my Sunday school kids" grow up, marry, and have children of their own!

One of the lessons I learned from feeling like the ugly duckling is to stop comparing myself to others. Galatians 6:4 says (NIV), "Each one should test his own actions. Then he can take pride in himself without comparing himself to somebody else." Why is it we always compare our weaknesses against someone else's strengths? For instance, we cannot carry a tune, and yet we compare ourselves with the worship leader. What kind of a comparison do we expect to get with that?—one where we always fall short! This is one of the tricks the enemy of our soul uses to make us feel unqualified to do the work God has called us to do. Through this, I discovered obedience to God brings self-worth. Exodus 19:5 (NIV) describes what we become as we obey God. It states, "Now if you obey me fully and keep my covenants, then out of all the nations you will be *my* 'treasured possession.'" I was not an ugly duckling, but instead I was and always have been God's treasured possession.

I also learned as I responded in obedience to God, He was and still is creating something graceful and beautiful in me and through my life.

Chapter 3

Higher than I Can Reach

Another area God spoke to me about was worrying. Worrying is the opposite of trusting. Worrying causes anxiety and steals our peace. First Peter 5:7 (NIV) declares to "cast all your anxiety on him because he cares for you." The practice of casting my cares on God would be a growing experience over a long period of time. To help facilitate that process, I decided to create a "prayer box." I wrote down the things I found myself worrying about: my health at the time, Richard's unemployment, needed car repairs, school clothes, and Christmas gifts for the kids. I wrote each worry on a piece of paper, put it in the box, and then wrote Philippians 4:6–7 (NIV) on the outside of the box. It reads, "Do not be anxious about anything, but in everything, by prayer and petition with thanksgiving, present your request to God. And the peace of God, which transcends all understanding, will guard your hearts and minds in Christ Jesus." I then prayed over each request, placed it in the box, and presented the box to God. Using a ladder, I placed the box out of my reach above the kitchen cabinets. Then every time I found myself starting to worry about something I had placed in the box, I would say out loud, "God, I cannot reach the box, if there is something I can do, I ask you to show me what it is, and then I ask you to do what I cannot do. I have placed my requests in your hands. Thank you for taking care of my concerns and giving me your peace." Philippians 4:6–7 (MSG) reads, "Don't fret or worry. Instead of worrying, pray. Let petitions and praises shape your worries into prayers, letting God know your concerns. Before you know it, a sense of God's wholeness, everything coming together for good, will come and settle you down."

What I have learned: (1) how easy it is to take back those worries we have given to God; 2) how wonderful it is when Christ displaces worry with his peace.

Chapter 4

Finding God's Calling

My parents became pastors of a small church that had been closed for years. It was in a farming town. They were excited when there were fifty people in attendance on Easter (a church's highest attendance is usually on Easter). Shortly after I married and left home, we joined them to help. Richard played the guitar. And because the church did not have a piano player, I was informed by my mother that I would learn the piano for services. I had ten accordion lessons as a child and could read basic music. I was so grateful the congregation was kind and forgiving as I learned to play the old hymns.

The organization was always looking for young people to encourage them into the pastorate. And if you were musically inclined, that was even better. After a few years of helping my parents, the organization and my parents encouraged us to try out for a small church with about twenty members in a small town in Idaho. By this time, we had two preschoolers. This organization allowed the congregation to vote in (and therefore vote out) the pastors. With prompting from the organization and my parents, we applied for the position of pastor. This entailed us "trying out" for the position by arriving early Sunday morning, me playing the piano and Richard preaching. Then there was a potluck with the congregation and the grueling questions, followed by an evening service with another sermon. The congregation would meet in private after the evening service and call the next day with their decision. On Monday, we eagerly awaited their phone call. It finally came late in the afternoon with the answer that we "were not what they were looking for as their pastor." Two months later, we heard they were still without a pastor and reapplied. This time they immediately replied without us "trying out." Again, we were told we "were not what they were looking for as their pastor." Two more months went by, and they were still without a pastor. Since we were the only couple to "try out," the organization called and asked us to take the church over the vote of the congregation. I knew that for us to succeed in this position, it would have to be God calling us. So I asked the organization if we could spend three days praying and fasting before we gave them an answer. They agreed.

I spent those three days in serious prayer and fasting before the Lord. At the end of the three days, God spoke to my heart, saying that He had not called us to the pastorate! At first I sighed a great sigh of relief. Then I asked the Lord, "If not the pastorate, then what was my calling?"

He said, "I want you to be putty."

Silly me corrected the Lord, "You mean clay. You are the potter, I am the clay."

At that He showed me a wooden floor much like a roller skating rink, only this floor had gaps between the boards and small chips out of some of the corners. Then he repeated himself, "I want you to be putty that fills in the cracks and the holes. Stay in a church, and do whatever the pastor over you needs to have done. That may mean cleaning the bathrooms and sanctuary or teaching a Sunday school class playing the piano or sharing words of encouragement. So that is what I have done to this day. Regardless what church God has placed me in, I have done whatever is needed.

Every pastor I have sat under has mentioned they wished they had more people who were "putty." Ecclesiastes 9:10 (NIV) declares, "Whatever your hand finds to do, do it with all your might." And Ephesians 2:10 (NIV) admonishes us: "For we are God's workmanship created in Christ Jesus to do good works, which God prepared in advance for us to do." God has a calling for your life!

What I have learned is to seek God myself for what it is he wants me to do and not let the pressure of other voices determine God's calling for my life.

Chapter 5

Little Is Much, Extravagant Giving

I remember the day well. It was a beautiful summer evening. We arrived at church for Sunday evening service. In tow were my three small children, my daughter who was six at the time, my son who was five, and a highly active two-year-old. We were a little early, which was very unusual as it took so much time to get the little ones ready. I took the opportunity to greet the others who had already arrived. As I shook hands with an elderly lady (I shall call Mabel), whom I considered a pillar in the church, she asked me, "Have you spent an hour in prayer and an hour in reading your Bible today?"

I remember thinking, *Oh, God, what I would give to be able to spend two hours a day in the Word and prayer!*

Of course my answer was no.

For three days after this conversation, I lived under condemnation and guilt that I was not a "good Christian" because I was not spending two hours a day reading God's Word and in prayer. Instead, my days were consumed by taking care of my husband and three small children. So many thoughts ran through my head during these three

LITTLE IS MUCH, EXTRAVAGANT GIVING

days. *Do I neglect my duties as a wife and mother to spend two hours a day in prayer and reading God's word? I did not even have time to go to the bathroom by myself. How could I even find that kind of time with meals, laundry, shopping, cleaning, baths, etc.?* The thoughts and feelings of failure brought this condemnation and guilt that I struggled with. Then one afternoon, the Spirit reminded me of the story in Luke 21:1–4 (MSG):

> Just then, he [Jesus] looked up and saw the rich people dropping offerings in the collection plate. Then he saw a poor widow put in two pennies. He said, "The plain truth is that this widow has given by far the largest offering today. All these others made offerings that they will never miss. She gave extravagantly what she could not afford—she gave her all!"

Then the Spirit spoke to my heart that the same principle is true of my time. Mabel was a widow without a husband, and her children were grown up and moved away from home. She had sixteen or more hours of time each day to give to God. Mothers of young children rarely even get to take a shower or sit on the toilet uninterrupted. The Spirit reminded me there were small bits of time, "pennies" if you will, that I was giving. I had written scriptures on the bathroom mirror in lipstick from sermons that had spoken to my heart so I could read and reread them while I brushed my teeth each morning. I wrote out scripture on paper and put them on the wall across the toilet so I could meditate on them several times a day as I did my duty. I also had scriptures above the kitchen sink to focus on while washing dishes. And I had my worship music playing as often as possible, which I would sing along to as I did my daily routine.

Romans 8:1 (NIV) says, "Therefore there is now no condemnation for those who are in Christ Jesus." And 1 Samuel 16:7 (NIV) declares that "the Lord looks at the heart." God saw my heart and my desire to give what I had. But I could not use this as an excuse to become lazy in my walk with God. I gave God what little time I had when my children were small. As they became older and able to do more things for themselves, this gave me the opportunity to give more time to God in Bible reading and prayer. Whatever you have, give it, knowing that little is much when God is in it.

The lessons I learned from this experience is that these little things were my "pennies" as an offering that God saw as extravagant gifts. Also, I learned not to allow others to make me feel guilty or condemned by them trying to fit me into what God was calling them to do or be.

Chapter 6

Affirmations

I have battled negativity most of my life. Listening to what others said made it worse. I remember one day, my mother was introducing us, three girls, to a friend of hers. She introduced Ann, and the lady said, "What beautiful eyes." She introduced Lou, and the lady said, "What beautiful hair." She introduced me, and the lady said, "So this is Loretta." I was hurt. At that time, I chose to focus on what I thought was an insult. I was tall for my age, skinny, and awkward.

According to John 8:44 (KJV), Jesus declares, one of the things the devil is, is a liar and the father of it. He bombardes our minds daily with lies. There is an old saying, you cannot stop a bird from flying over your head, but you can keep him from making a nest in your hair. As an adult, I wanted to change my negativity. How I did that is by focusing on Philippians 4:8 (KJV): "Finally, brethren, whatsoever things are true, whatsoever things are honest, whatsoever things are just, whatsoever things are pure, whatsoever things are lovely, whatsoever things are of good report, if there be any virtue, and if there be any praise, think on these things."

As I mentioned earlier, the Armor of God in Ephesians list several pieces, all are for our protection except "the Sword of the Spirit, which is the word of God" (Ephesians 6:17 KJV). It is the only weapon we have to defeat the enemy of our soul. I had to start paying attention to my thoughts. I did so by meditating on God's word. I had to break an old thought pattern. I had believed that meditation was just a "New Age," anti-God thing. Then I did some biblical research and discovered meditation is mentioned in several books in the Bible. In Genesis 24:63a, "And Isaac went out to meditate in the field at the eventide." In Joshua 1:8 (KJV), Joshua commanded the children of Israel, "This book of the law shall not depart out of thy mouth; but thou shalt meditate therein day and night that thou mayest observe to do according to all that is written therein: For then thou shalt make thy way prosperous, and then thou shalt have good success." In Psalm 1:1–2, it states, "Blessed is the man that walketh not in the counsel of the ungodly, nor standeth in the way of sinners, nor sitteth in the seat of the scornful. But his delight is in the law of the Lord; and in his law doth he meditate day and night." God's style of meditation is to fill your mind with the word of God. "New Age" meditation is to empty your mind.

I started praying, Psalm 25:5a (KJV), "Lead me in thy truth, and teach me: For thou art the God of my salvation."

God encouraged me to start writing affirmations of his word. I started out with writing verses about who God is:

God is love. (1 John 4:8 KJV)

God is not a man that he should lie; neither the son of man that he should repent: hath he said, and shall he not do it? Or hath he spoken, and shall he not make it good? (Numbers 23:19 KJV)

For the Lord thy God is a merciful God; he will not forsake thee, neither destroy thee, nor forget the covenant of thy fathers which he sware unto them. (Deuteronomy 4:31 KJV)

Know therefore that the Lord thy God, he is God, the faithful God, which keepeth covenant and mercy with them that love him and keep his commandments to a thousand generations. (Deuteronomy 7:9 KJV)

For the Lord your God is he that goeth with you to fight for you against your enemies, to save you. (Deuteronomy 20:4 KJV)

Be strong and courageous. Do not be afraid or terrified because of them, for the *Lord* your God goes with you; he will never leave you nor forsake you. (Deuteronomy 31:6 NIV)

The eternal God is thy refuge, and underneath are the everlasting arms. (Deuteronomy 33:27 KJV)

Have not I commanded thee? Be strong and of a good courage; be not afraid, neither be thou dismayed: For the Lord thy God is with thee whithersoever thou goest. (Joshua 1:9 KJV)

God is our refuge and strength, a very present help in trouble. (Psalm 46:1 KJV)

For this God is our God for ever and ever: He will be our guide even unto death. (Psalm 48:14 KJV)

When I cry unto thee, then shall mine enemies turn back: This I know; for God is for me. (Psalm 56:9 KJV)

Unto thee, O, my strength, will I sing: For God is my defense and the God of my mercy. (Psalm 59:17 KJV)

Trust in him at all times; ye people, pour out your heart before him: God is a refuge for us. Selah. (Psalm 62:8 KJV)

For the Lord God is a sun and shield: The Lord will give grace and glory: No good thing will he withhold from them that walk uprightly. (Psalm 84:11 KJV)

Gracious is the Lord and righteous; yea, our God is merciful. (Psalm 116:5 KJV)

I then started researching who God says *we* are. I found Ephesians chapters 1 and 2 to be full of amazing statements. We are

- chosen
- adopted
- beloved
- redeemed
- forgiven
- saved
- sealed with the Holy Spirit of promise
- quickened
- loved
- a holy temple and habitation of God

I needed to write these all out and tape them all over my house, so no matter where I was, I could meditate on them. They became my meditations and affirmations, truths that offered emotional support and encouragement. They have helped me learn to focus on the positive.

Chapter 7

Sharing the Reason for Hope

All three of my kids were now in school. I had the opportunity to attend the local community college. I applied for financial aid and started thinking about what classes I wanted to take. I thought the first quarter I would just take fun classes: pottery, beginning piano. However the financial aid did not come in time for the fall quarter, which gave me more time to think about what I should take. I asked Richard. He said it would be good to take some cooking classes. We had been married for eight years, and I did not like to cook. I thought if I knew what I was doing, maybe I would enjoy cooking. So I signed up for the culinary arts program. My financial aid came in time to start the winter quarter.

I had not worked since I married, just been a housewife taking care of the kids. I asked the Lord to give me the opportunity to witness while I was at school. Each day I looked for opportunities, but nothing opened. This went on for several months. One day in prayer, I asked God why. The next day in class, the pilot light went out on the gas stoves. I squatted down to light it. Another student yelled at me and told me to get up because I was in a dress. I told her I knew how to squat and not show anything. She yelled again, "Get up!" So I did and allowed her to light the stove.

The church we were attending at the time was very legalistic. Women were not allowed to cut their hair, wear makeup, nor wear pants. So I was wearing dresses to school every day while working in a kitchen.

Later that evening in prayer, I again asked God why there were no opportunities. He spoke to my heart and said I had set myself up on a pedestal, and fellow students thought if that is what Christianity is all about, they did not want any. I spent the weekend making myself two pairs of pants. The next week, I wore a dress on Monday, pants on Tuesday, a dress on Wednesday, pants on Thursday, and a dress again on Friday.

The following Monday, a fellow student yelled out that he needed a stiff drink.

I said, "No, you need God."

He yelled "I do not need religion."

I agreed and said, "No, you don't. You need a relationship with God."

It was one of those times in my life where I felt like I was looking from the outside, and the words were coming out of my mouth. I am sure it was the Holy Spirit. My fellow student turned and walked away. The next day, he approached me and wanted to go to church with me. Because of all the rules, I did not feel comfortable taking him to my church. I introduced him to another student who was a Christian and asked if he could go with him to his church, which he did.

The verse that came to mind was "And be ready always to give an answer to every man that asketh you a reason of the hope that is in you with meekness and fear" (1 Peter 3:15b KJV).

What I learned: (1) Do not shove Jesus down people's throats. I had a relationship with Jesus and shared that with him. I knew how religion was not the answer. (2) Once I pulled myself down off the pedestal and showed people I was not holier than thou, God opened many other doors to share my hope, and God has helped me. (3) Showing the love of God is what attracts the lost.

> Beloved, let us love one another: For love is of God; and everyone that loveth is born of God and knoweth God. (1 John 4:7 KJV)

Chapter 8

Vacations and Smiles

I was working at a local fast-food restaurant; my position was first assistant manager. This meant that I worked two opening shifts that started at 5:30 a.m. (because we served breakfast), a midshift from 11:00 a.m. to 8:00 p.m., and two closing shifts from 5:00 p.m. to 2:30 a.m. each week. I had been doing this for two years. My poor body did not know when to sleep. I pretty much came home, found something to eat, said hello to my three children, and went to bed. On top of the rotating shifts, I worked a total of sixty hours a week. Thankfully at the time, my three children were teenagers, so they could feed themselves, get themselves off to school, and do their own laundry.

At the end of my first year, I qualified for a one-week vacation (or forty hours), which I took one day at a time over the course of the year to turn two days off into three-day weekends. At the end of my second year, I qualified for two weeks off. We decided to take the two weeks off all at once and go camping. The first week, we spend in the wilderness area that had no facilities, sleeping in a sleeping bag in a tent. At the end of the week, I told Richard I could no longer stand sleeping with him in a sleeping bag. Sponge showers from the cold creek were just not doing the trick! We packed up and spent the second week at a nice campground with flushing toilets and showers that cost twenty-five cents for eight minutes, which I gladly paid.

Then Monday came, and it was back to work. In the fast-food business, crowds come in shifts and, usually, after I had sent someone home because it was too slow. (This was required to keep payroll in budget.) It was a beautiful summer evening when we had a rush of customers and were shorthanded, so I went back to the grill to help the cook. The rush lasted for about forty-five minutes. As soon as it was over, one of my employees who was working the drive-through, whom I shall call Shelly, approached me and wanted to know if she could make a comment. I had hired Shelly six months earlier. She was a detailed and customer service–oriented employee, so I readily said yes.

She said, "Loretta, you're smiling! In all the time I have worked here, I have never seen you smile!"

You could have knocked me over with a feather.

"Really?" I asked her.

My personality is bubbly and happy. How could she never have seen me smile? At that point, another employee chimed into the conversation. He had been working there since before I started, he mentioned that when I first came, he had seen me smiling a lot but had not seen me smile in an exceptionally long time. He said I was not grumpy, just focused. I realized later, he was trying to be kind.

I remember driving home that early morning, processing what I had just heard. This job had taken more than just a physical toll on me, it had changed me into someone

I was not. Maybe it was just the number of hours I was working, so I decided to talk to my supervisor the next day. When I went into work later that afternoon, I let her know I needed to cut my hours back to fifty a week. Her response was that she would do anything to keep me. When I came in the following day, my supervisor was crying at her desk. When I asked her why she was crying, she said, "Corporate told me to tell you sixty hours a week was what the job requires. You could take it or leave it. I know what you are going to do." She was correct. I asked for a piece of paper and turned in my two-week notice. The economy was much better back then, and I was able to find another job right away where I worked only forty hours a week. In this economy, I would have found another job before giving my notice.

In a poll from www.nydailynews.com from June 24, 2013, they state that 70 percent of Americans hate their jobs or are completely disengaged. This is not how God wants us to live. This may mean you take a test through the local college to find out what you are good at, if you need more education, take night classes and find that position that you enjoy. Remember in chapter 5, God has given you a gift! Ask him, and he will help you discover it.

What I learned from this is that no matter how much money I make (and this job at sixty hours a week salaried was not that great), it is best to have a job that I enjoy. Solomon, the wisest man, wrote in Ecclesiastes 3:12–13 (NIV), "I know that there is nothing better for men than to be happy and do good while they live, that everyone may eat and drink and find satisfaction in all his toil—this is the gift of God."

Section 4

Adult Children

Chapter 1

Give Them a Way Out

A dear friend of mine, whom I shall call Martha, had a daughter who lived clear across the country from her. I will call her daughter Missy. Missy had only been married about five years. They were living with her in-laws who did not care for Missy, and Missy's husband would not stop his parents from talking bad about Missy to her face, insulting her, or from treating her badly.

Missy called her mother on a regular basis, complaining about the situation and feeling depressed, like there was no way out. One evening Missy called her mother and was more depressed than usual. Her in-laws were getting meaner and meaner, making comments like "it was a mistake for our son to marry you. You are not good enough for him." Missy told her mother she had figured a way out. She would get in the car and drive to where there was a sharp turn in the road then drive straight off the road into the river. Martha made her daughter promise not to do anything for twenty-four hours. During that night, Martha sat in her rocking chair, crying out to God, feeling helpless with her daughter clear across the country. She said, "God, if only she were three again. I would be able to protect her." Martha then heard a whisper in her ear, saying, "Who protected your children when they were little? You were not there 24-7 to protect them. I protected them!" She knew it was the Lord. She asked God to protect Missy and give her wisdom to know what to say and do.

In the morning, Martha called me and shared the story. I mentioned to her that I have a friend who had attempted suicide. I suggested Martha and I call her. She agreed. My friend, whom I shall call Ruth, had turned her life around with God's help and was more than happy to share her story with us. She had gone to her pastor with her depression and thoughts of suicide. He had never dealt with someone with thoughts of suicide and did not know what to do or say, so he told her so and sent her away. At that point, Ruth felt that if her pastor could not help her, then there was no hope for her. So she sat up that evening, designing a plan of how she was going to commit the act. Back then there were not crisis hotlines or 2-1-1 numbers to call for help. Fortunately for Ruth, God came through, and someone found her, and she was rushed to the hospital. So she was unsuccessful in her attempt. While in the hospital, she was given the names and phone numbers of people who could help her. Her advice to us was to give Missy a way out, to buy her a plane ticket that would get her out of the situation long enough to think clearly. Martha and I combined funds to purchase Missy a plane ticket home for two weeks with the advice that she and her husband work things out over the phone during that time. By the end of the two weeks, her husband agreed to move them out from living with his parents so their marriage could have a chance. Missy flew back to help her husband move their belongings out of his parent's place. I am pleased to say, Missy is fine, and there have been no more attempts. She realizes how much her mother loves her, how much God loves her, and is thankful that He intervened.

Martha and I learned several things during this time: (1) from 2 Thessalonians 3:3 (NIV): "But the Lord is faithful, and he will strengthen and protect you from the evil one." The Lord had always been Missy's protector, Martha's protector, Ruth's protector, and mine as well, as he is yours and your children's protector; (2) when someone has a plan to commit suicide, *act quickly*! Never assume it is a threat to get attention; (3) from Proverbs 19:20 (NIV): "Listen to advice and accept instruction, and in the end you will be wise." We were so thankful for my friend Ruth and her willingness to not only share her story but to give us suggestions as how to help.

Chapter 2

Acknowledging God

Since God knows what the next year holds for me, I ask Him at the end of each year to give me a Bible verse or a word to hold onto during the coming year. One December I heard Him prompt my heart with Proverbs 3:5–6 (KJV): "Trust in the *Lord* with all thine heart, and lean not unto thine own understanding. In all thy ways, acknowledge him, and he shall direct thy paths." So I did as I often do. I wrote it on the bathroom mirror in lipstick. I knew this verse well. I had memorized this verse as a child. However I did not know what it really meant until the following year.

It was early spring when I received the news that I was going to be a grandmother. Ordinarily, this would have been wonderful news a few years later, but the kids were only seventeen years old. I had married the first time just one week after I turned seventeen, and my daughter was born just before I turned eighteen. I knew how difficult being a young parent was. You grow up awfully fast the hard way.

A week after receiving the news, my son's girlfriend informed us, she wanted nothing more to do with him or us and had not told her mother she was pregnant. I informed her mother who was a nurse. And she insisted her daughter have the baby and give the baby up for adoption. We hired an attorney. But back then, fathers did not have the rights they have today. We were told he would have to pay child support, and he and us, as grandparents, would only have limited visitation. We were devastated. This was my son's first child and our first grandchild.

I remember coming home from work a few days later and reading Proverbs 3:5–6 on the bathroom mirror. I remember crying out, "Lord, I don't understand this! How can *you* be in this heartbreak?" Over the next two months, I struggled with why God would allow me to be a grandmother and only allow me to be a small part of the child's life. I am so thankful for God's grace and mercy in dealing with me during these times. One afternoon I heard the Spirit prompt my heart with "Trust in the Lord! In all your ways, acknowledge him (God), and he will direct your path."

Okay, God, I get it. I am supposed to acknowledge that you are in this. I took a deep breath and said, "God, I don't know how you are in this, but I confess that you are. I will trust you. Please show us what to do. Please direct our steps."

Within a week, we were contacted by an adoption attorney and received word that the now ex-girlfriend was giving the baby up for adoption, and that my son would need to give his permission for this to happen. He and I made an appointment for the following week to see the attorney and discuss what this really meant. When we arrived, we were told a family had already been chosen to adopt the baby. We could view their application and information. They had been married fifteen years and could not have children. They were Christians who attended church. The woman was a schoolteacher, and the man owned his own successful business. We asked the attorney if it would be possible to meet them, if it could be an open adoption, and if we could hold the baby when it was born. He said he would have to ask the adoptive parents and would give us a call as soon as he had an answer. Knowing this was in the best interest of the baby, my son gave his permission for the child to be adopted. It was two weeks later before we received a phone call back from the attorney. The answers were, yes, we could meet the couple; yes, it could be an open adoption; and *yes*, we could hold the baby when it was born. There were still four more months before the due date. During that time, I kept busy crocheting a baby afghan to give my first grandchild, and my son purchased a large stuffed dog to give as well.

On December 14, we received the call, she was born. We could come to the hospital the next day to meet the adoptive parents and hold her. As we were sitting in the waiting area, I purchased a travel cup, and every time I used it, I would pray for her. It was a day mixed with great delight and great sorrow. I was able to hold my precious granddaughter, and pray for her, then put her into someone else's arms and walk away.

We were delighted in the spring to receive our first letter with pictures of her baptism and heartfelt letter, thanking us for giving them this wonderful blessing, this precious baby. The letters came each year with pictures. And as she started school, we received artwork she did as well as her report cards. God truly did direct our path and still allowed us to be part of our first grandchild's life. She has now completed seminary and has her PhD. She wants to serve God in the ministry! She is an amazing woman, and I was privileged to hold her in my arms again just a few years ago.

She invited us to her ordination, which we were able to attend. I am privileged to hear her sermons on Sundays via Facebook. God was able to do what Romans 8:28 (KJV) declares: "And we know that in all things, God works for the good of those who love him, who have been called according to his purpose." God never said everything that happens to us would *feel* good, only that in *all things*, he would *work it* for our good.

I learned to acknowledge God in *every* circumstance. Yes, God is in whatever dark and sad time we go through. Recognize that God is in this with you, and watch as God directs your steps.

Chapter 3

The Christmas Tree

It was a crisp fall Saturday when we drove our daughter 150 miles to set her up in her dormitory room her freshman year of college. It was a bittersweet moment leaving her there that afternoon, my first child out the door and on her own. I was proud of the choice she had made to attend a Christian college but also felt grief in my heart.

This was also the same year my seventeen-year-old son, who had just graduated high school, had his first "real" job, not just a part-time job but forty hours a week that paid him above minimum wage. As Christmas approached, he asked me what I wanted most for Christmas. I told him, for years I envied all my girlfriends that had coordinated Christmas trees, where the ornaments were all matching. Money was tight when my children were growing up, so we made ornaments to hang on the tree or looped different colored paper strips or strung popcorn and cranberries to use as garland. When my son asked me what colors I wanted my coordinated Christmas tree to be, I excitedly exclaimed, "Silver and blue!" On his next payday, he went out and purchased all kinds of silver and blue decorations and gave them to me for an early Christmas gift. He and I spent that next Saturday decorating the tree. When we finished, it was so beautiful! And I was so proud of my coordinated Christmas tree, I could hardly wait to surprise my daughter when she came home for Christmas break.

However the surprise was on me. As my daughter walked into the living room and saw the beautifully coordinated Christmas tree, she dropped her bags and burst into tears. When I finally calmed her down enough to talk, she said, "Mom, I was just bragging to all my college friends that every year you put the ornaments we made as children on the tree." She felt as though I had broken an old family tradition. I had no idea how important it was to her to see their handmade ornaments on the tree. Upon realizing the preciousness of this tradition, I unselfishly removed all my "coordinated ornaments," and my daughter and I spent the afternoon redecorating the Christmas tree.

Fifteen years later, my son shared with me how devastated he was when I removed the "coordinated ornaments" from the tree he spent his hard-earned money on. I was heartbroken to discover this. I thought I had taken them down as an act of unselfishness only to discover I had hurt him. I apologized to him, and he so graciously forgave me.

I have since learned: (1) Seek God's wisdom regarding matters in life that appear to have only one-way-or-the-other solutions. James 1:5 (NIV) declares, "If any of you lacks wisdom, he should ask God who gives generously to all without finding fault, and it will be given to him." James 3:17 (NIV) explains, "But the wisdom that comes from heaven is first of all pure then peace loving, considerate, submissive, full of mercy and good fruit, impartial and

THE CHRISTMAS TREE

sincere." (2) My original decision was considerate of my daughter's feelings but not my son's. It showed partiality to my daughter and did not consider how my son would have felt. (3) A few years ago, God gave me His wisdom, a three-way solution in the Christmas tree situation I thought had to be one way or the other. Since that time I have put my silver and blue ornaments on the Christmas tree right next to the ornaments of my children and now grandchildren have made, I had also put my Christmas Village my son and I painted under the tree to honor him as well. Now my Christmas tree is full of wonderful memories for all my children and grandchildren.

Chapter 4

The Gift of Time

As I mentioned earlier in the book, I was one of five children, plus Mom took in foster kids before there was a program. What that meant was there was little one-on-one time with Mom. When I became a mother, I chose to purposely make time with each of them. When they were little, I chose to stagger their bedtimes by a half an hour. I did not send my children to bed; I put them to bed. I started with my youngest at 8:00 p.m. Once in bed, I "tucked him in," sat on his bedside, and read him a story, or we would talk about the day. At 8:30 p.m., I gave him a kiss and did the same with my older son. At 9:00 p.m., I put my daughter to bed. She was about third grade at that time. I was able to do this for several years until I started working swing shift.

When my schedule prevented me from putting each child to bed, I had to find other creative ways to spend time with them. I started taking one child at a time to the grocery store with me creating special one-on-one time. This also helped save my sanity. Walking through the grocery store with all three children, saying, "Mommy, can I have?" drove me a bit crazy. (And many days, it was a short drive!) Each child was given the condition that if they did not ask for anything during our shopping time, we would stop by the ice-cream store on the way home. Sometimes I had to remind them of their reward. As we sat and ate our ice cream, we talked about what was happening at school and with their friends. This worked well until I forgot who went with me the last time! Then I started writing on the calendar whose turn it was next. This avoided the fighting and gave me one-on-one time I so desired with each of my children. I was not only giving each child the gift of time with me, I also enjoyed the gift of time with each of them as they grew up.

Those who know me well will tell you I am constantly doing something. Part of my busyness was because I was a business manager and supervisor for over twenty years. In the business world, we are taught to make use of every minute to be the most productive. As a business manager, I carried a Day-Timer just to see how much I could get done in a day. One day a friend of mine had observed I ran late to most of my meetings. She said that was because I had too much on my plate! I had not given that much thought. When she said that, I realized she was right; I almost always showed up ten to fifteen minutes late to every meeting. As I pondered her statement, it began to bother me. I realized my being late was disrespectful to others, so I asked God to help me respect other people's time by being on time. Just a few weeks later, my precious pastor preached a sermon on "giving yourself the gift of time." He pointed out that when we schedule ourselves tightly, there is no room for life's interruptions, like roadwork we were not expecting or when God redirects our path. I then began to evaluate my schedule and to think about what was important for me to do or if someone else could do that task. This meant I had to learn a new skill of saying *no* instead of yes to everything. Overscheduling leaves no room for God to intervene in our day for us to minister to someone else. Overscheduling also causes unneeded stress in our lives. From then on, I would get up each morning and ask God to guide my day with a determination to follow his leading. I realized that is what the Lord's Prayer is about. Matthew 6:10 (KJV) says, "Thy kingdom come, thy will be done on earth as it is in heaven."

One afternoon my friend and I decided to go shopping. Before I left my house, I asked the Lord to have his will in my life that day. We had been shopping at a couple of different stores, and we were heading home when we came across a single woman whose car was stranded in the middle of an intersection. My friend and I pulled over to help her push her car out of the intersection, but it would not budge. Then Paul, a mechanic who attended my church, saw me and came to the rescue. He immediately knew her car's transmission was locked up and found the release button. When he pushed the button, we were then able to move her car to safety. The next Sunday, Paul told me the only reason he stopped was because he had seen me. What if I had not given myself the gift of time or had been too busy about my own schedule? I would have missed an opportunity to bless someone else.

What I learned is (1) to give my children, and now my grandchildren, the gift of my time and (2) to give myself the gift of time to be available for the will of God in my life.

Chapter 5

Seeing God

Have you ever desired something so badly that when the time came, and it did not happen, you were actually heart-sick? Was it that job you knew you were going to get or that man you thought you were going to marry or that baby you have been waiting and praying for? I have felt that pain, that "deep down in your heart and soul" sadness. I remember crying out to God, saying, "Lord, do you hear the cry of my heart? Where are you?" The longing of my heart was so deep, and the aching was unbearable, I felt as if I was living in darkness. I asked myself where was God during this time.

    The Spirit reminded me of a time when Moses wondered where God was. You can read the story in Exodus chapters 32–33. The Israelites had been delivered out of Egypt through the miracle of God parting the Red Sea then closing the sea upon the Egyptian army. They were now in the wilderness. The first thing the children of Israel did was to complain about no water. God provided water for them. Then they complained about no food. God provided manna for them every day. Then they complained about no water again. And again, God provided water for them.

God knew that for the children of Israel to survive in their new world, they would need guidelines, so God called Moses up onto the mountain of God where God, with his own finger, hewn out the Ten Commandments. While Moses was conversing with God, the children of Israel convinced Aaron to make a golden calf for them to worship. Now get this, God had miraculously provided water and food for two-and-a-half million people!

God tells Moses to go down and deal with the people. When Moses saw them dancing around, naked before the golden calf, he became angry and threw down the tablets of stone the Ten Commandments were written on and broke them into pieces. God's anger was against all the children of Israel, and He thought to slay them all. God sent a great plague, and many of the Israelites were slain that day. This experience discouraged Moses's heart.

In chapter 33 (vs 21–23), Moses went into the temple to seek God. In the Message Bible, Moses cries out to God, saying, "Let me in on your plans. Are you traveling with us or not? Let me see your Glory." He was discouraged by how the very people he was to lead to the promise land were behaving. How many times in the midst of our trials, we want to see God and know He is with us in our darkest times? God spoke to Moses, saying, "Look, here is a place right beside me. Put yourself in this rock. When my glory passes by, I will cover you with my hand until I pass by. Then I will take my hand away, and you will see my back. But you won't see my face."

Psalms 91:2 (NIV) says this, "God, you're my refuge. I trust in you, and I'm safe!" Solomon, the wisest man, declares in 1 Kings 8:12 (KJV), "Then spake Solomon, 'The Lord dwells in the thick darkness." He is in the darkness with you and me. A pastor I sat under for a long time used to say, "God's delays are not God's denials. God may be silent, but *he* is not idle!" He is working on your and my behalf in the dark times. Keep trusting God. Proverbs 13:12 (KJV) declares, "Hope deferred maketh the heart sick: *But* when the desire cometh, it is a tree of life." The scripture did not say *if,* it says when. Keep trusting God. He is working in the thick darkness of your life, and you will be able to see what He has done *when* you walk out of the darkness.

What I learned is that (1) he is right beside me even when I do not feel him; (2) that I am protected in the cleft of the rock; (3) that I am covered with his hand; and (4) that I will know he has been there all the time when the darkness is over, and I see what he has done as he walks away. If he showed his face while we were in the midst of the darkness, there would be no need to trust God.

Chapter 6

What Do These Stones Mean?

I love it when God speaks to my heart through pastor's message. This is an incredibly special message as it prepared me for what lies ahead.

Pastor read this passage about the children of Israel having to cross the Jordan River before they could enter the Promised Land:

> And tell them to take up twelve stones from the middle of the Jordan, from right where the priests are standing, and carry them over with you and put them down at the place where you stay tonight. So Joshua called together the twelve men he had appointed from the Israelites, one from each tribe, and said to them, "Go over before the ark of the *Lord* your God into the middle of the Jordan. Each of you is to take up a stone on his shoulder according to the number of the tribes of the Israelites, to serve as a sign among you.

WHAT DO THESE STONES MEAN?

> In the future when your children ask you, "What do these stones mean?" tell them that the flow of the Jordan was cut off before the ark of the covenant of the *Lord*. When it crossed the Jordan, the waters of the Jordan were cut off. These stones are to be a memorial to the people of Israel forever. (Joshua 4:3–7 NIV)

At the end of the message, the pastor asked each of us to come to the front and take a stone out of a basket. (They were about the size of silver dollars.)

"Take one home," he said, "pray over it, and think about a time when God did something amazing during a time when you felt like you were between a rock and a hard place. Then write one word on the stone as a reminder." I waited to be closer to the end of the line to go up and realized there were extra stones, so I took two.

That afternoon in prayer, two words came to my mind: "faithful" and "strength." So I wrote them on the stones.

It was not even a month, while I was living with my daughter and two teenage granddaughters, that my daughter was having female problems. She had gone in for some tests, and we were waiting for the results. The phone rang, it was the doctor's assistant. She asked my daughter her name then told her the test results revealed stage 4 ovarian cancer. Our lives changed at that moment. It felt like the rug had been pulled out from underneath us, and we fell flat on our faces. We had so many questions. What were we going to do? Would I be raising two teenagers? She did not have insurance, how were we going to pay for treatments? That evening I saw my two stones next to my bed and was reminded of the faithfulness of God and that he is our strength. I was reminded of Jeremiah 16:19 (NIV): "*Lord*, my strength and my fortress, my refuge in time of distress," and "I can do all this through him who gives me strength" (Philippians 4:13 NIV). With God's strength and faithfulness, I had the confidence we were going to make it through this Jordan.

For the next thirty days, we researched natural ways that could help my daughter. And we spent over $2,000 on home remedies, but she did not seem to get better. So she decided to call her doctor to see what other options there were.

When he returned her call, she asked him, "What's next?"

He asked, "Regarding what?"

She informed him of the test results his assistant had given.

The doctor told my daughter, "Your test results were that you have a very bad infection but not cancer."

The doctor then researched and found out his assistant had given my daughter the test results for someone else with the same name. We were relieved and angry. That assistant did not confirm my daughter's birth date. However, we were praising God for no cancer.

What I learned: (1) So many times, God gives me what I need just before I need it; (2) God gave me a new perspective with compassion on how people feel with that kind of a diagnosis. It is heartbreaking and life changing. My prayers went out to the family of the other woman whose results did show cancer. I was so thankful for my stones that reminded me God was my strength, and he is faithful!

Section 5

Endings or Beginnings

Chapter 1

Heartbreak

Because when you marry, two truly do become one. When you divorce, it is like your heart is ripped in half. You feel like your life has ended. It is hard to just get out of bed and put one foot in front of the other. I wanted to cry all the time, but the only safe place I felt I could cry was at church and curled up in the fetal position in the bathtub. There were days I wondered if God even heard my cries. I am thankful for the Word of God and his promises.

As I talked with others who had endured divorce, I realized divorce is a grieving process. But unlike the death of a spouse, people usually do not come around you to grieve with you or bring you comfort. Even though over 43 percent of marriages end in divorce, many churches still treat divorcées like they have the plague. One of the most devastating things that happens in divorce is when friends you have both known choose to take sides. I remember lying in bed, sobbing so hard my chest hurt because my long-time "friends" chose to believe the untrue statements my ex was spreading. I was most thankful for the few who stood with me during this grieving process. I told God at that time that I did not want another man in my life, just me and Jesus. I went out and bought a fake diamond ring and called it my me-and-Jesus ring. It helped keep other guys away.

One of the things I learned from this experience is that God did hear my cries. Psalms 107:28 (KJV) states, "Then they cry unto the Lord in their trouble, and he bringeth them out of their distresses." Psalms 61:2 (KJV) tells us what to do when we are overwhelmed. "From the end of the earth will I cry unto thee, when my heart is overwhelmed [crushed], lead me to that rock that is higher than I"—the rock, Christ Jesus. "The Lord is close to the brokenhearted and saves those who are crushed in spirit" (Psalms 34:18 NIV). I was not alone!

The other thing I learned was to focus on the future. This was difficult as I had been married for thirty-three years, I was still in high school, a senior, when we got married. I had thirty-three years of married memories. So I had to decide to purposely work at making new memories with my children and grandchildren. To help with this, I meditated on Philippians 3:13b–14 (NIV): "But one thing I do: Forgetting what is behind and straining toward what is ahead, I press on toward the goal to win the prize for which God has called me heavenward in Christ Jesus."

I had to learn to stop retelling the hurtful memories and work hard at making new memories. This took effort and time. Only two of my children lived locally. My daughter, who had been through divorce herself, stayed open and kept our relationship active. However our son, because he had Richard living with him, who was telling our son his strictly one-sided stories, was not extremely interested in keeping our relationship going to gain empathy from our son.

A couple of years later, I invited him and his family over to open Christmas gifts. I spent several days in prayer, asking God what gift to give him. I believe God inspired me to put together a box of all the things I used to put in the kid's stockings when they were little. While shopping for those items, I saw a fishing tackle box full of gummy worms. I had learned he had taken up fishing recently. When he opened the box, there was a big smile on his face, it was the most wonderful memory. I am happy to say God has restored that relationship.

One of the things I learned was that had I not continued to work on restoring my son's relationship, it would have died. And I had to stop retelling myself the negative memories and start creating new positive memories.

Chapter 2

The Opposite of Love

I remember thinking I still loved Richard a year later even though I did not feel loved by him in the relationship. One day the Holy Spirit asked me what the opposite of love was, and like most people, I said hate. Then the Spirit reminded me of John 3:16 (KJV): "For God so loved the world that *he gave* his one and only Son that whoever believes in him shall not perish but have everlasting life." Then a light came on, God loved us so much he gave, therefore, God shows us the opposite of love is selfishness. First Corinthians 13:4–7 (NIV) states, "Love is patient, love is kind. It does not envy, it does not boast, it is not proud. It is not rude, *it is not self-seeking*, it is not easily angered, and it keeps no record of wrongs. Love does not delight in evil but rejoices with the truth. It always protects, always trusts, always hopes, and always perseveres."

One of our greatest examples on earth is of a mother's love. I remember giving my mother chocolates for her birthday or Mother's Day, and she would share them with everyone in the house. It used to upset me. I would tell her, "I bought those for *you*." But she had such a giving heart.

At my mother's memorial, I shared a story of our mother. The family was waiting in the waiting room at the hospital while my mother was undergoing some tests. The doctor walked out and said, "Well your mother has a good heart!" Little did he know how true that statement was. She was always helping other people. We often had other children living with us. She did this before there was even a foster care program. Several times, two brothers and a sister lived with us. Their mother would drop them off. Then when her current relationship broke up, she would come and pick them back up. There was a baby we had for several months. He was a chunk, we called him Sherman Tank. Then there were three young girls whose mother died the beginning of summer. Their dad still had to work but could not afford a babysitter. So Mom kept the girls all summer long. Yes, my mother had a good, loving, unselfish heart.

What I learned is that true love is not selfish, marital or parental love.

Chapter 3

Not a Waste!

I remember the day well; it was a hot autumn day. I was mad at the world. It had been a little over three months since the divorce was filed, and it had just been finalized. I was walking out of the courthouse into the heat, shouting at God, "What a waste! What a stinking waste! A thirty-three-year marriage dissolved! What a waste!" But God, in his mercy, reminded me at that time, I had three grown children and eight precious grandchildren I would not have had if it were not for that marriage.

As I got into the car, God whispered to my heart that Moses thought the same thing, wandering the desert for forty years. The lessons he learned in the desert he would use bringing the children of Israel through that same desert. Second Corinthians 1:3–4 (NIV) states, "Praise be to the God and Father of our Lord Jesus Christ, the Father of compassion and the God of all comfort who comforts us in all our troubles so that we can comfort those in any troubles with the same comfort we ourselves have received from God." God was preparing Moses to lead the children of Israel through the desert. My journey was so I could lead others who were going through divorce to God.

I Remember that first Christmas as a single woman. I had lost my faith. I believed God put Richard and I together, so why had everything fallen apart? I have since discovered that marriage is the process of two people working together toward the same goal. If goals are different or if only one person is working at it, marriage does not work.

Many divorcées battle depression the first year. Psalm 42:5 (KJV) states, "Why art thou cast down, O, my soul? And why art thou disquieted in me? Hope thou in God, for I shall yet praise him for the help of his countenance." It was a rough first year, however God brought me through it. We had a family tradition of meeting at a local restaurant on Christmas morning for breakfast. I had to start new traditions, they helped me through the years.

In Jeremiah 31:13 (KJV), God declares, "I will turn their mourning into joy and will comfort them and make them rejoice from their soul sorrow."

One of the things I learned is that (1) Christ desires us to be the victor not the victim. "No, in all these things, we are more than conquerors through him who loved us" (Romans 8:37 NIV). God spoke to my heart just as Moses led the children of Israel through the wilderness. I would help other women through the wilderness journey of divorce. It would not be a waste. (2) As children of God, I learned no circumstances are accidental. Psalm 37:23 states (KJV), "The steps of a good man are ordered by the *Lord*: and he delighteth in his way." Usually, God orders our steps to help others in their walk as God has helped us.

Chapter 4

Lost Identity

It is so common to be in financially dire straits after divorce. It was six months before I had money to go out and eat. Who am I? What do I like? I had poured myself into others and lost who I was. I decided to go to a restaurant we used to go to all the time. It was an all-you-can-eat buffet. I remember sitting, eating, thinking I did not like the food here. It took several months of trying new restaurants and discovering what food I liked.

And discovering my identity, I am who the scriptures say I am:

> I am honored in the eyes of the *Lord*, and my God has been my strength. (Isaiah 49:5b NIV)

> But I am like an olive tree flourishing in the house of God; I trust in God's unfailing love for ever and ever. (Psalm 52:8 NIV)

> I no longer call you servants because a servant does not know his master's business. Instead, I have called you friends. (John 15:15a NIV)

> See what great love the Father has lavished on us that we should be called children of God! And that is what we are! (1 John 3:1 NIV)

Many of us did not have loving, protective fathers who provided for us or took care of us. I struggled with God as a Father for many years until I began to see all the ways he lavished his love on me. I did not begin seeing this until I was single, and God provided for me repeatedly. I remember lying in bed each evening, counting the many blessings God had bestowed upon me that day. For a while, I worked on writing down five things a night I was thankful for. This helped me keep my focus on God.

What I learned was to focus on being thankful to God daily. This helped me focus on God's love and care for me and helped to see I was God's blessed daughter.

Chapter 5

Forgiveness

It was not an easy thing for me to do, to forgive. I was encouraged to follow Jesus and Stephen's example in Luke 23:34 (MSG), "Jesus prayed, 'Father, forgive them, they don't know what they're doing.'"

One thing that has helped me let go and forgive others is to say, "They did the best they could with the knowledge they had at the time." This was especially helpful forgiving my dad for his failure to provide, care for, and protect us children. Because he was an alcoholic and mom would not let him come home when he was drunk, He would take off for weeks or months. He himself did not have a particularly good childhood and did not surround himself with other good fathers. I remember a Father's Day play at church, shortly after he became a Christian. They had another father play the part of the father who ignored his child, and my father, the one who picked up the child, hugged her, and solved the problem. I remember thinking in my nine-year-old mind, "They have the daddies mixed up." Seeing a Christian therapist has helped me work through forgiveness and my abandonment issues.

I remember after my dad's passing, my mom asked me to go put flowers on Dad's plot. I was uncomfortable doing so. But to honor my mom, I did. As I stood at his plot, I remember yelling, "You did it again, Dad, you left Mom to take care of things!" After I got home, I called my cousin, who was a hospice chaplain, and told him what just happened. He asked me if I knew why I had said that. I told him that I had some abandonment issues. He agreed.

There is much in the Bible about forgiveness. This is how Jesus taught us to pray, "Forgive us our debts as we also have forgiven our debtors. For if you forgive men when they sin against you, your heavenly Father will also forgive you. But if you do not forgive men their sins, your Father will not forgive your sins" (Matthew 6:12, 14–15 NIV).

> Forbearing one another and forgiving one another, if any man have a quarrel against any: even as Christ forgave you, so also do ye" (Colossians 3:13 KJV)

"Grudge not one against another, brethren, lest ye be condemned: behold, the judge standeth before the door" (James 5:9 KJV). Grudge is a secret malice or ill will based on *past* offense or grievance.

I wish I could say forgiving others was easy, it was not for me. My therapist helped me on several levels. For some people, I wrote letters, outlining what they had done; and how it had affected me. Most I burned. One I did send and broke off a relationship with that person because they could no longer be trusted. I refused to put myself in harm's way again.

What I learned was when it comes to other people, God never commanded us to trust people; he commanded us to love, forgive, and pray for people. He commanded us to trust *him*. Others must prove themselves worthy to be trusted.

Paul gives us an outline of how we are to pray for other believers in Colossians 1:8–11.

1. We are to ask God to fill them with the knowledge of his will through all spiritual wisdom and understanding.
2. We are to pray that they may live a life worthy of the Lord and may please him in every way.
3. We are to pray that they may bear fruit in every good work.
4. We are to pray that they may grow in the knowledge of God.
5. We are to pray that they may be strengthened with all power according to his glorious might.
6. We are to pray that they may have great endurance and patience.
7. And joyfully give thanks to the Father for them. (MSG)

Even though Richard claimed to be a Christian, I had my doubts based on his behavior. He had spread many untrue statements. I wanted to pray Proverbs 28:10: "He shall fall himself into his own pit." However, I knew God was asking me to pray the Colossians prayer for him. It was not without struggle. There were some days it took everything I had to obey God. So thankful I did, forgiveness brought my healing. I have recently heard in a sermon that harboring unforgiveness is like drinking poison and expecting the other person to die. It only hurts you, not them. I then came across this verse in John 20:23 (MSG): "If you forgive someone's sins, they're gone for good. If you do not forgive sins, what are you going to do with them?"

Chapter 6

God's Provisions

One of the darkest times in my life was when my thirty-three-year marriage ended in divorce. Not only was this an emotionally difficult time, but it was also financially dark. But as I look back, I can see how God provided for my needs.

The divorce papers were served on Thursday, July 7. Because Richard had been unemployed for over a year, we had wiped out our savings to pay monthly bills. I was working, and he was not. I took my check and made his truck payment, his insurance payment, and his cell phone payment to give him time to find a job to pay his own bills. There was no extra money, and I would not receive a paycheck for fourteen more days. There was no food in the house. I made too much to qualify for state assistance but not enough to make ends meet. On Friday, the very next day, a friend heard about the divorce and invited me out to lunch. Just being with her meant a lot to me, but the bonus was the leftovers I took home for dinner. On Saturday, my precious daughter-in-law called me and invited me out to lunch as well. She had been through divorce and knew I was in shock and denial. What a great help she was just being there. Again, there was enough leftovers for dinner Saturday night.

Later that evening, my brother called. He knew I would not be comfortable attending the same church Richard and I had attended together for twenty-five years. My brother was coming in to town Sunday morning and invited me to attend the church he used to attend when he lived in town. I looked forward to seeing my older brother. He was a 6' 6" tall man, and he intimidated most people. But when people became acquainted with him, they realized he was just a loveable teddy bear. I cried through most of the church service that day. After service, the pastor announced there was a potluck, and everyone was invited—ah, lunch! After the potluck, my brother walked me out to my car and handed me a check for $200. I started crying again and told him I had no money until I received my next check in eleven more days. His gift would pay my car insurance and cell phone bill.

I went back to my apartment, lay on the bed, overwhelmed with a heart full of thanksgiving for the provision of God when someone knocked on my door. It was my friend Patty whom I had known for ten years. She lived in the same apartment building and attended the same church as I had. She asked if I would help her unload some things from her car. I said yes and went outside with her. When we got to the car, she opened the trunk, which was loaded with food. She then informed me she had gone shopping for me! The food filled my refrigerator, my freezer, her refrigerator, and her freezer. I know she spent hundreds of dollars. Her only request was that I would cook one meal a week for us to eat together. I told her I would cook dinner every night for her! We ended up eating together about three times a week. That food lasted us over three months! I am sure God multiplied it! Not only was the food a blessing, but her company was also. She too had been through divorce and understood the emotional and financial journey.

During that first year, I took on all the bills that were in both of our names to protect my credit. Because of this, I had become accustomed to going without many things to keep the bills paid. I put into practice trusting the Word of God. Philippians 4:19 was the verse I stood on during that year (NIV): "And my God will meet all your need according to his glorious riches in Christ Jesus." It was a time when I came to realize what a need was and what a desire was. As I walked through that dark year, I learned the importance of giving thanks to the Lord as Psalms 92:1 (KJV) declares, "It is a good thing to give thanks unto the Lord and to sing praises unto thy name, O, most High." As I looked back over that first year as a divorced woman, I could truly see where God had not only carried me but how friends and family supported me. Never underestimate what your time, hug, love, and gift can do to help someone going through divorce.

Chapter 7

Deciding to Go to School at Fifty-Five

I had been thinking about going to college but had not discussed it with anyone. One day a friend brought a newspaper clipping to my office. The clipping discussed a program a local college offered called PLA, giving college credits at a reduced cost for life experiences. I found the thought remarkably interesting, so I attended a free seminar on how the program worked. I discovered you pull up the learning outcome for the class, then write a paper sharing your experiences that have taught you those outcomes. It was graded by a professor who taught that class. And if you prove you knew the outcomes by your experiences, you were then given credits for that class. I signed up and started two weeks later.

The amazing thing about going to college after not being in school for forty-eight years is that so many of the professors would often tell me they liked what I wrote. As this continued over months, it empowered me to do my best. I started my "big girl college word list," trying to stop using three-letter words and building my vocabulary. I also had a friend I paid $25 a paper to edit, which also helped my final papers look so much better and increased my vocabulary as well. It was so worth it. I worked full-time and attended night and weekend classes; therefore it took me seven years to obtain my bachelor's degree.

I had many moments where I wanted to throw up my hands and quit.

I learned to surround myself with friends and family who believed in me. They encouraged me and reminded me that "I can do all things through Christ who strengtheneth me" (Philippians 4:13 KJV). Knowing this, I kept pressing on.

Chapter 8

Closing the Door on the Past

I was taking some coaching classes. We were doing peer reviews, and I was complaining to a fellow student about how I felt unable to close the door on my past. He asked me what my married name was. When I told him I had not changed it, he suggested it was what was holding me back, since it had been seven years since the divorce. So I decided to go home and search the Scripture about name changes. This is what I discovered.

Bible characters whom God changed their name:

1. Abram to Abraham, meaning the father of many—this was after Ishmael was born but before the promised child was conceived.
2. Sarai to Sarah, meaning princess, before Isaac was born
3. Jacob to Israel, meaning wrestled with God and has prevailed
4. Saul to Paul, meaning humble

My first thought was to go back to my maiden name. However there were some family members who had been arrested, and I did not want to be associated with them. My daughter-in-law suggested I choose a new name, quoting the verse: "One thing I do: forgetting what is behind and straining toward what is ahead" (Philippians 3:13 NIV).

Since I had been collecting swans for years, I chose Swan, one full of grace and beauty. I paid to have my name legally changed at the courthouse. It could have been free with the divorce. My excuse for keeping my married name at the time was that we had eight small grandchildren, and I did not want to confuse them. I later realized it was just my denial.

Changing my name was powerful! It was the beginning of my journey to start straining forward and not to keep focusing on my past. Another thing that helped me move forward was to stop telling the hurts of my past. Every time I would tell someone of my story, I would relive it. It helped me to make new memories with my children and grandchildren.

Chapter 9

The Kids

Our children were grown adults and had children of their own when the divorce happened. The two oldest had gone through a divorce themselves, so they were supportive of both of us. However, it was exceedingly difficult for our youngest, mostly because he had allowed Richard to move into his home. Richard used this opportunity to tell our son all the things he thought were wrong with our marriage over the years and blamed me for them. This put a wall between my tenderhearted son and myself. His wife would often call me and tell me what Richard had said. It was heartbreaking for me. At one point, I had to ask his wife to stop telling me anything about Richard.

Psalm 56:1 states how I felt, "Be merciful unto me, O God, for man would swallow me up; he, fighting daily, oppresseth me." I remembered 2 Chronicles 32:9a: "With him is an arm of flesh; but with us is the Lord our God to help us and to fight our battles."

I knew I could not insist my son hear my side of the story as it would just cause more harm than good. I asked God to help me. I decided to invest in my son's relationship. My son's birthday was just a month after the divorce was final. I showed up at his work, just before his shift started, with a cake to share with his coworkers and a gift for him. This brought a smile to his face and great delight to my heart. Each year that passed, I made sure to mail him a birthday card, an anniversary card, and a Christmas card. These were ways to acknowledge him and my love for him.

Three years later, I wanted to do something more and asked God to help me. I invited my son and his family over to give them a Christmas gift. After much prayer, I believe God gave me an idea—to fill the box with items I used to put in their stockings as children. As I was at the store purchasing these items, I noticed a fishing tackle box filled with gummy worms. I also purchased that as I had heard he had recently taken up fishing. He and his three girls had fun opening the box filled with goodies, but the biggest smile on his face was when he picked up the tackle box. Seeing his smile brought great joy to my heart.

God has restored our relationship. In the last couple of years, I have been invited over to their home for dinner. Richard had married and moved out. Rebuilding the relationship with my son has taken time and patience, as well as resisting to fight, allowing God to fight for me. it was so worth the results.

Lamentations 3:26 (KJV) states that "it is good that a man should both hope and quietly wait for the salvation of the *Lord*."

Section 6
Africa

Chapter 1

Like That Will Ever Happen!

In 2005, I took on a challenge to sponsor two children, Angel and Emmanuel, in Rwanda, Africa. At that time, the cost was $25 each a month. With the sponsorship, the children can attend school, are given a meal while at school, books are provided as well as a uniform and shoes, also medical attention if needed.

The church I attended sends a group of volunteers each year to help maintain the school in Rwanda. In 2006, Angel discovered the team was there from my church. She began asking the team members if I had come. When she was told no, she sat down and wrote me this letter.

> Greetings in the Name of the Lord. When I heard the team was from your church, I asked if you had come. I was saddened to discover you were not here. When are you coming? I want to meet you face-to-face. Love, Angel.

LIKE THAT WILL EVER HAPPEN!

When the letter arrived, I read it, and I laughed out loud, saying, "Like that will ever happen!" I threw the letter on the table and started walking away. Then the Holy Spirit asked, "Why not?" I begin making all kinds of excuses. I am single. I have a dog to take care of. It is dangerous out of the country. It costs too much money. I do not have a passport.

I decided I would go talk with my pastor who surely would say, it is too dangerous for a single woman. So I made an appointment.

When I explained my concerns, my pastor responded by saying, "Sis, I think it would be a perfect fit for you to go, and my wife and I will help with your support"—so much for excuses. So I went to the next meeting for those interested and started the process of obtaining my passport. I told God he would have to supply the funds as it would cost $4,000. I was happily surprised to find extra bonus money on my quarterly checks. I also sent out a sponsorship letter and saw some money come in that way as well. I ran across an article that said it was easier to get $1 from 1,000 people than $1,000 from one person. So I am sure God gave me the idea to bake cookies and sell them for $1 a bag off my desk. We also had a fundraiser dinner that helped everyone who was going. By the time it came to leave, I had all my funds.

What I learned was when I stopped making excuses and was obedient to what God was showing me to do, he provided the ideas and funds to make it happen.

Chapter 2

Opposition

At the fundraising dinner, I was sitting across from Emmanuel Sitaki Kayinamura, founder and president of Rwanda Rise, the guest speaker who was a survivor of the Rwandan genocide. I mentioned I would be going and desired to leave something behind for my children and their families. He asked what I had in mind. I told him chickens and a large bag of rice.

He informed me, "Chickens do not survive the summers in Rwanda, but a pair of goats would."

I asked him, "How much would a pair of goats cost?"

He said, "$35."

I could do that!

I was so excited about buying goats, I started telling my friends and family. And without asking others, they started giving me $35 to buy a pair of goats from them.

At one of the info meetings to prep us for the trip, I was informed by someone who had been to Rwanda before, I needed to stop talking about the goats because they could not be purchased for $35 a pair.

I had been keeping track of everyone who had given me money for goats and decided if I could not find the goats, I would return their money with a thank you card when I arrived back home. But I would take the money with me and see what God would do.

The next morning after we arrived in Rwanda, there was a knock at the hostel door. It was a local pastor. He was told I had been raising money to purchase goats for $35 a pair and was told to tell me that was impossible, which he did. The amazing thing was that I kept my mouth shut.

I have learned that many times, when God is in something, there is always opposition. But opposition does not mean to stop. Keep pressing onward.

Chapter 3

Katie's Missing Suitcase

We left the US on Thursday morning. We spend forty-eight hours on planes or waiting on transfers at airports, wearing the same clothes. When we landed in Kenya, we had to walk out on the tarmac and identify our luggage to be put on the final flight to Rwanda. One couple brought their two small children. And while their mom was attending to their needs inside the airport, she asked her husband to go out and identify their luggage. When we arrived late Saturday evening at the Rwanda airport, it was discovered that their eight-year-old daughter Katie's luggage had not arrived. They called the Kenya airport and discovered it was still sitting on the tarmac. We went ahead to the hostel, and Katie was crying all the way there. She was not to be comforted. She did not have her pajamas, her stuffed bear, or her blanket.

She must have cried for over an hour when God reminded me of something in my suitcase. I asked her mom what size she wore. She said, "An 8." I ran upstairs to my room. I had purchased a couple of dresses for Angel for $2 each, and there were some more on the rack in a larger size. I had purchased them also. They were a size 8. I ran them downstairs and asked Katie if she would like to do a fashion show for us. She stopped crying and ran into her room with the dresses to change. She came back out wearing a dress with a big smile on her face. At that moment, God put a thought in my heart to share with her.

"Sweetheart", I said, "before you even knew you had a need, God had me purchase and pack these dresses in my suitcase, so they would be here when you needed them."

The next day, we went to go see the child Katie's parents sponsored. Her mom had also brought their little girl a gift. We all laughed when their child opened their gift. It was the same dress Katie was wearing that I had bought and given her.

What I have learned is God has often reminded me he has the answers before we even know we have a need. "Your Father knows what you need before you ask him" (Matthew 6:8b NIV), and Isaiah 65:24a (KJV) states, "And it shall come to pass, that before they call, I will answer."

Chapter 4

Emmanuel's Story

Our third day in Rwanda was spent at the street kids feeding program where children who are homeless come three times a week to receive a large plate full of rice, covered with peanut gravy for protein.

The other four days of the week, they rummage through garbage to find food. The facilities where they receive their rice plate is also the same facilities where sponsored children write letters to their sponsors. The head of the sponsorship program, Sara, invited me and another couple to tour the facility. We, of course, accepted her invitation.

While we were in the room where our children wrote their letters, Sara asked me why I had come to Rwanda. I told her I had been invited by one of my children. She asked me who they were. I told her Angel and Emmanuel. She asked Emmanuel and stated his last name. I told her I did not know his last name, only his number was 0074. She exclaimed, "You are Emmanuel's sponsor!"

Sara then explained his story. They never tell the children they have been chosen to be sponsored until the first check arrives, which, in my case, was good because I chose Emmanuel and Angel when our house was put on the market after the divorce. Unfortunately, it did not sell for four months. That was when I was finally able to mail off the first check. When the check arrives, they go to the child's home to inform the parents the child has been sponsored and will be able to attend school. When they knocked on the door and Emmanuel's mother opened it, they found Emmanuel lying on the dirt floor, his stomach extended. He was dying from worms. They scooped him up, took him and his mother to the hospital. They used my first check to pay the doctor, purchase the needed medicine for him, and had enough left for a large bag of rice. While they were waiting for the doctor to see Emmanuel, his mother told Sara, when they knocked, she was praying, asking God to save the life of her child. All I could say was, "My little $25, my little $25."

The next month when my check arrived, they went to check on Emmanuel. He was still too weak to attend school, so they took my check and purchased beans, rice, and oil to help him gain his strength. By the time the third check arrived, he was well enough to attend school. Sara said, "I will make sure you are able to meet Emmanuel and his family, and Angel as well." She did. Three days later, we went to the school. I was able to hold Emmanuel in my arms, give him the gifts I had brought for him, and spend time with him and his family. I asked his mother if they had a place to keep a live goat. The interpreter said they did, so I gave the organization the money to purchase them one. I was able to hold Angel in my arms, give her the gifts I brought for her, and spend time with her and her mother. As our van was pulling away from the school to head back to the hostel, I could hear Emmanuel screaming my name. It was hard leaving that day. I did not see him again before we flew home. But every year, the organization would send pictures of the children; and in one of them, he had his goat on a leash.

What I have learned is that even though I thought my checks were late, they arrived just in time to save Emmanuel's life. So I try not to stress when things do not happen when I think they should. This reminds me God is always on time.

Chapter 5

Finding Goats

The next to our last day in Rwanda was set aside to visit the genocide sites. I am too tenderhearted and informed our leader I could not go. He told me I would never understand the plight of the Rwandan people if I did not go. I told him, "I could not." After much debate and me standing my ground, he finally agreed to allow me to stay behind and watch the children. I was fine with that.

After everyone left, there was a knock at the door. It was Emmanuel Sitaki Kayinamura, founder and president of Rwanda Rise. He did not remember me from the fundraising dinner six months earlier, but I remembered him. I invited him in, the children were napping. We sat down, and I asked him why he was in Rwanda from the states. He shared his heart about helping widows become self-sufficient by starting businesses. I asked what kind of businesses. He said some wanted to learn how to sew so they could sell garments in the market. Others wanted to learn how to farm and sell their vegetables in the market, as well as eat them. And then he said, others wanted to start a goat farm, to sell the milk and baby goats for income.

I stood up and yelled, "I have goat money!" I ran upstairs and got it. Part was in US dollars and part was in Rwandan. It took him a little time to calculate it out. Once he figured out how much was there, he said we had enough to purchase twenty pairs of goats. He told me, "Tomorrow you and I will go find the goats." The next morning, he knocked on the door. The team thought he was there to be their interpreter for a day of shopping until he told them he and I were going to find goats.

It took us a few hours to find the goat farm. By then the only person who could take the money was gone to lunch. We came back later that day, and he was gone for the day. We were given permission to look at the goats. I held several baby goats in my arms.

baby goat

It was so thrilling to see how God had pulled it all together. We were not able to purchase the goats or take them that day. Emmanuel would have to go back the next day after he dropped us off at the airport. That evening when other team members heard, we found goats for $35 a pair. They gave Emmanuel more money. I asked Emmanuel to take pictures when he picked them up and send them to me to share with all the people who provided money to purchase them. And he did. After dropping us off at the airport, he went back to pay for the goats. The workers at the goat farm started loading the goats into the van he had driven us to the airport in. Emanuel tried to tell them he would return later with a truck, but they insisted he take the goats then and kept loading them.

goats in van

We started out with twenty-four pairs of goats. Seven years later, there were five hundred goats on this farm supporting widows and orphans. Little is much when God is in it.

And Jesus looking upon them saith, "With men, it is impossible but not with God. For with God all things are possible." (Mark 10:27 KJV)

And he said, "The things which are impossible with men are possible with God." (Luke 18:27 KJV)

What I learned and am still learning: (1) Nothing is impossible with God. I did not solicit funds for the goats. God provided the funds. And now widows and orphans half way around the world have a thriving business providing for their needs. (2) I also learned to keep my mouth shut and let God fight the battle.

Chapter 6

The Flight Home

We were halfway home when one of the team members who had been to Rwanda several times said, "I am glad I am not a mother in Rwanda."

I asked, "Why?"

She said, "During the genocide, women were raped and purposely given AIDS. Now if they become pregnant, the baby is born AIDS-free unless she is in the final stages. Once the baby is born, she must decide whether to breastfeed the baby, which will give the baby AIDS and give a death sentence, or not feed the baby and allow it to starve to death."

For over a week, that statement haunted me. When I saw my teammate at church the next Sunday, I told her, "This is not a choice any mother should have to make. Could we get bottles and formula over there to give them a better choice?"

She informed me I had no idea how much that would cost. And it would be stopped by customs, and fees would be charged to pick it up—not possible.

Not again, I thought. *Had she not seen God do the impossible?*

A month later, our pastor's wife mentioned how goats' milk would work—what a brilliant idea! There are goats there already. For the next few years, I researched and wrote papers at school. Kenya already has tried this with great success. It would work with a $300, one-time gift that would purchase baby bottles, a lactating goat, and two thermoses to keep the goats' milk fresh all night or all day, a nurse to help the mother learn how to use them, and to make sure there are no medical issues with mother or baby. The nurse would check in weekly at first, then monthly for the first two years.

What I have learned is that I do not know how God is going to bring this to pass. I am willing and waiting to see this impossibility become a possibility.

Section 7

Moving Forward with a Push

Chapter 1

Some Things Are Worth Fighting For

Growing up, we were not allowed to fight. If we did, we would be disciplined. This caused me to learn to walk away.

One day I was let go from a job. I was given no opportunity for correction or improvement. It was devastating. I was going to walk away from fighting for unemployment. My boss had fought my unemployment, and I was sent a denial letter. I felt a prompting in my heart that I believe was the Holy Spirit: "If you don't fight, I can't bring you the victory." But I did not know what to do. The Spirit reminded me of James 1:5 (NIV), "If any of you lacks wisdom, you should ask God who gives generously to all without finding fault, and it will be given to you." I asked God to help me. He reminded me there were phone numbers on the bottom of the denial letter. I called them, and they gave me some immensely helpful information, certain words to use and codes also. They informed me there would be a hearing with a judge, my boss, and myself via a conference call. I prayed, "Lord, help me. I have this phone meeting with the unemployment judge, and my ex-boss in two days. I have done the research. Now I am asking for divine intervention and wisdom as my ex-boss has already stopped my unemployment once. God, you know he is an ex-attorney. I will do my best to be prepared. God you must do the rest. Thank you for hearing my cry. Amen."

I spent two days preparing thirteen pages of documents to send over to the judge. By the end of the conversation, the judge had made her decision. My ex-boss told another employee he had won. But God came through! My unemployment was approved, including the eight weeks he had fought, and I had not been paid for. I was able to catch up on my bills. And later I found out that 75 percent of people who fight their unemployment win! I know it was God working on my behalf.

I learned to ask God for wisdom when I do not know what to do and to do my best, then leave the rest to God. First Corinthians 3:9a (KJV) states, "For we are laborers together with God."

Chapter 2

Buying My Trailer

My daughter, Ann, no longer needed my financial assistance because God provided for her because she was now receiving monthly checks, she suggested I look for a manufactured home and use my retirement money to purchase it. I did not have very much in my retirement account, but I did have some money. If I used it to purchase a manufactured home, then all I would have to pay was the space rent and utilities.

My daughter-in-law suggested buying in a senior's park. So we started looking around. Ann and I drove from one park to another and finally found a senior manufactured home park. I stopped by the manager's office. She had two homes for sale but not within my price range. She did mention there was a trailer in the park that was for sale by owner I should go look at. We stopped and knocked. There was no one living in it, just a sign in the window with a phone number. I called the number, and the woman said she could come over after work and let me look around. We met her and went in; it needed a lot of work. In the bathroom, two things had swans on them: a hand towel and a powder dish. They were special to me. The trailer had belonged to her mother who had died in a care facility, and the kids did not want anything to do with it. So they were selling it. It was within my price range with enough money left to do the repairs. I got a money order and sealed the deal. Ann and I started fixing it up. Ann has an interior decorating degree. So it turned into an extremely cute "dollhouse."

Here is the before picture before any work to it.

After the work was done.

What I learned is to listen to advise from others and then go looking. It was God who opened the door to be able to buy it. My daughter and I put a lot of sweat in it. And as you will see in the next chapter, God's timing was perfect again!

Chapter 3

The Fall I Will Never Forget

We had spent several weeks working on my trailer, getting it ready to move in. When my sister called and informed me, she would be moving to Idaho from Washington. Her husband was already there working and would be unable to help her pack. I drove up Friday night, and we spent the night planning on how to pack the moving truck. We were both so thankful the rain had stopped that evening.

Saturday morning, I got up. My sister said we would start with the garage, and I should park my car in the vacant lot next door and back it up to their driveway. I felt like I should put my dog in my car to keep him out of the way. As I was approaching my passenger side door, I slipped on the wet grass, one leg going out in front of me and the other underneath me. I heard the bone snap. As I fell on the ground, my dog ran under my car. I started yelling for my sister. She was still in the house and evidently could not hear me. I thought I would try standing up to see if I could put any weight on it—bad idea! I could not. About that time my sister came outside, she was on the phone. I got her attention by yelling. I broke my ankle. She hung up and came over helping me get into her pickup. Then she went back and got my dog out from under my car. She drove me to the ER. I had broken the bone just above my ankle.

The doctor set it in a cast and told my sister she would have to help me for the next few days.

I told the doctor, "I had come to help her."

He said, "Not happening now."

My sister called her husband who came back home to help since I was not going to be able to. I stayed with them for a week.

I called my daughter to let her know what happened. She called some of our friends who helped her move my furniture from her third-floor apartment, where I had been living with her, to my trailer. There was no way for me to climb her stairs. My trailer had a ramp to the front door that I could maneuver on crutches. I was so thankful to God for the trailer. I was reminded of Romans 8:28: "We know that all things work together for good to them that love God, to them who are called according to his purpose." God did not promise that everything that happened to us would be good, but he would work everything (good or bad) together for our good.

What I learned: 1) Buying the trailer was God's perfect timing. 2) How wonderful it is to have friends who rallied around to help me get moved in.

Chapter 4

Helping Hands

I was unable to work for five months with no income coming in. Since I had paid for the trailer, the only housing bills I had was the three-hundred-dollar-a-month space rent and utilities. Once again, God provided. I would have church friends come pick me up in my wheelchair and take me to church. Many times, people would give me handshakes with money in their hands. My daughter-in-law came over two days in a row and spent both days making meals, putting them in individual serving containers, and stocking the freezer. This kept me fed for over two months. After a couple of months, I applied for food stamps and was approved. By that time, I was able to do my own cooking.

I started receiving bills from the hospital and the doctors. A friend of mine told me I could write the hospital and doctors and explain my situation and ask them to write off their bill. I did that. God provided, and they all wrote the bills off. I was so thankful! I was also told to contact the electric company. They needed proof of my situation. A friend of mine drove me down there; I gave them what they needed; and they gave me a grant to cover my past months' bills and a little credit for the next month.

On several occasions, family and friends stepped up to help me out. One day a friend called, saying she was on her way to pick me up, not saying why. She picked me up, and we took a drive up the river to a place where there were several waterfalls. It was a beautiful day. The sun was shining. It felt so good.

Once I came out of church to find someone had slipped a hundred-dollar bill through the sunroof of my car. It was sitting on my car seat. I had locked the car so that was the only way they could have gotten it in my car. It was just in time to purchase groceries and gas. By that time, I was driving myself.

What I learned: how good it is to reach out to others when they are going through difficult times. You never know how much your acts of kindness could encourage someone. "Therefore encourage one another and build each other up, just as in fact you are doing" (1 Thessalonians 5:11 NIV). I would not have been able to survive those five months without the help of friends and family. Sometimes it was money; sometimes it was time; and sometimes it was information, all of which were a blessing to me.

Chapter 5

Sowing Seeds in the Midst of Drought

One time a friend picked me up for church and then took me over to her place for lunch. While she was fixing lunch, she had the Christian TV channel on. One pastor was sharing something profound. I wish I could remember who it was. He had an apple he had sliced. He passed the slices out to some people in the front row. Then he asked them to bite where the seeds were. The camera focused on their faces as they bit the seeds. He asked, "Is it bitter?" They responded with sour faces. Then he gave some other people on the front row more slices without seeds. They had smiles on their faces as they bit into the fruit. He then began preaching, how so many people are eating the seeds God gave them to plant, and life is bitter. If you want a crop, start planting those seeds even when you feel money is tight. Then enjoy the fruit when it ripens. This really hit home for me. "A man reaps what he sows" (Galatians 6:7b NIV). I had to ask myself if I was even sowing anything. No planting seeds, no harvest.

The next Sunday, someone else picked me up for church, and afterward we went to a restaurant for lunch.

Before we got out of the car, I tried giving my friend $5 to help with gas. She did not want to accept it because she knew my financial situation. I then told her about the sermon from last Sunday, and I wanted to plant seeds. She finally accepted it. Someone else from church also showed up at the same restaurant and ate lunch with us. As we were leaving, the other person handed me $20. I mentioned to the driver how God had already brought a harvest! "Remember this: Whoever sows sparingly will also reap sparingly, and whoever sows generously will also reap generously" (2 Corinthians 9:6 NIV).

I learned to sow if I wanted a harvest. Even small seeds can produce a harvest.

Chapter 6

Running Out of Money to Finish School

Because I was only attending school part-time, it was taking longer to get my degree than the four years most people do it in. I had already spent five years working toward my degree. One day I received a call from the financial aid office telling me I had capped out my student loans.

"What do you mean I have capped out my student loans?" I asked.

She said there was no more money for me to borrow to finish my degree.

"But I still have two to three years before I graduate," I retorted.

She apologized, suggested I go ahead and file for more financial aid, saying, "You never know what might happen." And she hung up.

I was reminded I had finished a certificate, so I at least had something. However, it looked like I was not going to complete my degree. I decided to make an appointment to talk with someone in the admin office to see what else I could do. The person I spoke with was not very encouraging.

He said, "We do not keep money around here to help people who have used up their funds."

As I left the school that day, I cried out to God.

"What now, God?" I asked.

I had no idea what was ahead, to come this close to my degree and not achieve it. I was heartsick. Then I remembered this verse: "Hope deferred makes the heart sick, but a longing fulfilled is a tree of life" (Proverbs 13:12 NIV). This verse encouraged me to keep hoping.

What I learned is that we are not always given all the information we need up front. Even so, I still put the problem in God's hands.

Chapter 7

Provisions to Finish School

I felt like the Holy Spirit prompted my heart to follow her advice and apply for financial aid anyway, which I did in the spring. I received a letter the beginning of summer informing me I had been approved for a small loan but not enough to pay for part-time classes. The beginning of September, a month before classes were to start, I received a phone call asking why I had not returned the financial aid paperwork. I told the person in the financial aid office it was because the loan was not enough to cover my classes, and I could not come up with the difference to stay in school. She said she was sorry to hear that and hung up. Two weeks before school was to start, I received another call from the financial aid office. This time it was an answer to prayer. I was being offered a presidential scholarship.

I asked, "Between the scholarship and the loan, would it cover my classes?"

She said, "Yes."

So I signed up for classes. As it turned out, it was $50 short, but I could cover that and my books. God made a way where there seemed to be no way.

I remembered this verse: "For I the *Lord* thy God will hold thy right hand, saying unto thee, Fear not; I will help thee" (Isaiah 41:13 KJV).

What I learned: (1) to step out in faith and apply for financial aid anyway; (2) to give my problem to God. I was able to finish school and graduate with my bachelor's degree.

Chapter 8

My Yearly Word

Each December, I ask God for a Bible verse or a word to encourage me throughout the next year since only he knows what the next year holds. This last year, my Bible verse was Matthew 1:23 (NIV): "They will call him Immanuel" (which means "God with us"). One of the definitions for "with" is a person accompanying another for protection—how appropriate for 2020 with the pandemic and the unrest in our country. We are not in this alone, God is with us!

I am an extravert. I gain energy from being around others. And this staying at home, sheltering in place has been extremely hard for me. I am thankful for being able to enjoy our Sunday morning service virtually, including the worship time. I can text my grandchildren, but I miss being with them in person. I used to enjoy going shopping with my granddaughters, having lunch together, and getting our nails done. I look forward to the day when we can meet in person and give each other hugs.

I try to get out on my patio when the sun is shining. I keep the blinds open during the day to let in whatever sunshine there is. I have two elderly neighbors and a single mom I check on regularly, keeping social distancing. I have given them my phone number to call if they need anything. We have also donated to our church where they are giving food boxes out to the needy. That helps with my desire to give and make a difference.

Even though I cannot be around others, I know God is with me, and I am not alone.

> Have I not commanded you? Be strong and courageous. Do not be afraid; do not be discouraged, for the *Lord* your God will be with you wherever you go. (Joshua 1:9 NIV)

Isaiah 43:2 (KJV) brings such comfort: "When you pass through the waters, I will be with you."

Another year, God gave me part of Isaiah 9:6 (NIV): "And he will be called wonderful counselor." This verse helped me through a difficult year when I needed guidance in several areas of my life. One was for a job I needed. I was asking God for his wisdom. My daughter called one day and said I needed to take a break from job seeking, which I had been at for several weeks straight. She suggested window-shopping. We met at a place she really enjoyed going to. We had been checking out what new merchandise had come in for about an hour when they announced over the loudspeaker that they were having a hiring fair upstairs. I told my daughter, "I have my resume out in the car, I will go get it." They interviewed me on the spot, told me of one position in the returns department. The next day, they called and offered me a different position with a higher starting wage, taking care of customer service calls. I was able to start work three days later.

This is the same time I looked up Philippians 4:19 (KJV) to stand on for my needs: "But my God shall supply all your need according to his riches in glory by Christ Jesus." I remember reading it and thinking, *God, I have more than one need.* I had been raised that it said "needs."

Then the Spirit spoke to my heart and said, "I will provide the source of income" (which he did). It is your responsibility to be a wise steward. I did some research and found a man who had designed a Christian budget that included giving to church and others. I started working on becoming a better steward. This took some time as a budget must be personally tailored. For the first several months, I had to keep track of spending, which I did by asking for receipts on everything I purchased then entering them into a spreadsheet and adjusting the budget accordingly. This also helped me see where I was overspending. A budget is never a one-size-fits-all. However, I remembered hearing Zig Ziglar once say, "If you aim at nothing, you will hit it every time." God truly is a wonderful counselor. Psalms 18:32 declares, "It is God that girdeth me with strength and maketh my way perfect."

What I learned: (1) how important it is to seek God for his insight for the coming year, only he knows what the next year holds; (2) how important it is as a single person to become a wise steward.

Chapter 9

Saying Yes to God's Will

Classes started the end of September. I had my books and was ready to work toward finishing my degree. I needed a math class and an elective class, I chose "Art of the Beginner," thinking it would be an easy class alongside of my more difficult math class. However the instructor believed art was hard work, and she was going to prove it to us. There was only one other person in the class of thirty that I knew, she was one of my previous instructors. As weeks went by, the homework and work in class got harder and harder. One evening after my math class, I went into the library to do some research when a fellow student from the art class approached me and asked me if I was having a hard time in the class. I said yes. We chatted for a few moments, then Eric told me he was also having a hard time. He said he would like to talk to me some more but had to get back to work. I thought that was an offer to meet, so I asked if he would like to get together after work for coffee and to talk some more about class. He said yes. I panicked and left the building. I then called my daughter and said, "I think I just asked someone out on a date." She assured me going out for coffee to discuss class was not at date. I felt better. He walked into the office area and told his boss he just got asked out on a date, which I found out months later. We did meet after he got off work and talked about the frustrations of the art class for over an hour. We then met every week after class for the entire quarter to talk about the class. It was his senior year with a very heavy class load.

The second time we met, I had already determined to find out if he was a Christian as I had watched family and friends stay in relationships where the other person was not. They all ended badly. If he was not, I had already determined to stop going to coffee with him. I was happy to discover he was, and he attended the same organization I grew up in and where I gave my heart to God. As I got to know him, I learned he had lost his wife to cancer ten years earlier. He had been her caregiver. Now he was his mother's caregiver. He had a heart of helps. After the quarter was over, we started "dating," going out to dinner, to plays, museums, and for long walks. However, before we started dating, I made it clear, there would be nothing physical. I had learned from Richard, a relationship built on being physical was not a good foundation. It had to be built on friendship and unselfishness. We did not even hold hands until May 18, we had been dating for five months. May 18 was when I introduced him to my children. We did not kiss until his graduation, the middle of June.

By the end of June, we both realized we were falling in love. It scared me so bad, mostly because of my first marriage. I planned on hopping in my car with my suitcase and my dog and driving away. That evening while in prayer, God asked me if I wanted his will or my own. I told him

I had already tried my own will with Richard and did not want to go down that road again.

He said, "Stay put!"

So I did.

July 4, our date was a long walk on a trail alongside a creek. There was a bench that overlooked the creek where we sat to rest. While we were sitting, a butterfly landed on my knee. I was afraid to move. It was so beautiful. It stayed there for several minutes. After it flew away, we went and bought a picnic and had lunch.

On July 7, we went back to the same trail and walked again. No butterfly this time, however we crawled down to the creek and sat on the large rocks, watching the water and listening to the birds. It was so peaceful. Then Eric said he did not know what my middle name was. I told him. He then called me by my full name and asked me to marry him. I said yes. We went back to the car to talk and make plans. I took off my me-and-Jesus ring when Eric gave me his engagement ring. That was July of 2013. We were married that September, just before my sixtieth birthday.

I am reminded of Jeremiah 29:11 (NIV): "'For I know the plans I have for you,' declares the *Lord*, 'plans to prosper you and not to harm you, plans to give you hope and a future.'"

What I learned: (1) to make sure Eric was a Christian; (2) to set boundaries when it came to being physical while dating; (3) to not panic but listen to God and say yes to his will.

Chapter 10

The Case of Full Disclosure

I wanted to make sure our relationship was built on being honest with each other. Eric knew about my broken ankle, but he did not know I had been out of work for over five months and was currently only working part-time. I had three past-due bills that had gone to collections. I wanted to make sure he knew where I stood financially. After sharing that with Eric in the restaurant parking lot, he drove me home but then did not call me that night. He had been calling me every night even if we had spent the day together. I was sure it was over. I remember praying, "God, your will be done." That was a little more difficult to say now that I knew I was in love. The next afternoon, Eric called and said we needed to talk. He had a plan. Up to this point, I thought he was just a poor college student, living off work-study. He then decided to be up-front with me and told me he had just inherited money from his father's passing a month before we met. He would like to pay off my debt so we could start our life together debt-free. What an amazing, unselfish act of love. I was honored and humbled.

I had been single for nine years, and he had been single for ten. We had both taken that time to work on our self, to become a better person so we could be a better mate. We had also both told God we would wait for the person he had planned for us. Because we were both obedient to God and decided to go to college, later in life, that was where we met. God only shows me one step at a time. (For me, the first step was to start school; for Eric, it was to finish his degree he had already started.) As we were obedient to take that step, then God showed us the next step. (For me, it was to apply for financial aid when it seemed impossible and staying put when God told me to.) That is how God leads me. He usually does not give me a five-year plan, only a step at a time. Psalm 119:105 (NIV) states, "Your word is a lamp for my feet, a light on my path." Have you ever been camping and walking on a trail at night? The flashlight shines just in front of you, taking each step one at a time.

What I learned: (1) It is best to have a relationship that is based on trust and being open with each other. (2) While we were single, we both worked on becoming a better person, which in turn would make us a better mate. (3) God only shows me one step at a time, taking that first step is always a step of faith.

Chapter 11

Can You Hear Me Now?

Eric and I were engaged. He had been seeing his doctor about a hearing loss. I started having hearing problems and mentioned it to him one day.

He said, "I am taking you to see my doctor."

I replied, "I do not have insurance."

He responded, "I did not ask you that."

He called and made an appointment for me.

We arrived at the doctor's office. A few minutes later, the doctor's assistant came out and said, "The doctor wants a urine test. I do not know why he wants a urine test for a hearing loss, but that is what we are going to do."

She escorted me back to the lab room. When I was finished, she escorted me to the next available room to wait for the doctor. Upon his arrival, he glanced through my file and asked where the hearing test results were. I mentioned we had not done a hearing test. Then he called his assistant, she reiterated she thought he asked for a urine test.

He said, "*You* need a hearing test!"

She took me to the room to perform the hearing test. Then back to the room, the doctor had waited for me there.

He informed me we had a problem. There was sugar in my urine. He had some blood test taken. We would not know the results for a few days.

I received a call a few days later to come in to the office. At this time, he told me my A1C glucose count was 14.3, this is an extremely high number. He said I was diabetic and probably had been for a long time. Because I did not have insurance, it had not been previously discovered. I did not know what the symptoms were. I thought being very thirsty all the time was just because it was summer.

I was still in college. I did not have Wi-Fi at home, so I would go to a local fast-food restaurant and order a large sweetened iced tea and do my homework there. They had free Wi-Fi I could use if I purchased something. I believe it was God who had the wrong test taken, otherwise I would not have known to start doing something about it—learning to like unsweetened iced tea, paying more attention to what I ate, less sweets. My most recent A1C is 7.6, under better control. "Where does my help come from? My help comes from the *Lord*, the Maker of heaven and earth" (Psalm 121:1b–2 NIV). I did not even know I needed help.

What I learned: (1) Even when I did not know I had a medical problem, God intervened and saw to it the wrong test was taken to discover it. (2) Once this was brought to my attention, I was then given the information I needed to get my number under better control, although I was still the one who had to change my diet.

Chapter 12

Miracles

I had been working for this company for about six months. It was the most difficult position I had ever had. It was with an international company. They did not have any understanding of how to work with US employees. Many times I had seen coworkers get written up without supervisors checking the facts. During the six months I was there, more than twenty people quit. I had two weeks of training, then my trainer was sent to another store to help with their grand opening. No one was assigned to complete my training, which should have taken two months. The stress level was extremely high as the company had no tolerance for learning from your mistakes.

I answered phones and solved customer complaints. I worked from 4:00 p.m. to 10:00 p.m., Tuesday through Saturday. Each evening during dinner, I would call Eric, my husband, and talk with him. It was December 31. Before dinner, I had been on the phone with an upset customer. He seemed to get more and more agitated. Finally he yelled at me and said he could not understand me, would I speak a little slower, which I did. We were able to work out a solution to his problem. Then it was break time. I called Eric and asked him to pray for me as I was having a difficult night.

After break, I had to go down two flights of stairs to get a signature from a supervisor. As I was walking down the stairs, my leg went out from in front of me. Fortunately, I had both hands on the hand rails, so I did not fall. The rest of the night seemed to just drag on. Finally, 10:00 p.m. arrived, and I drove the five miles home.

I was so tired; I went straight to bed. At 3:00 a.m., I woke up to go to the bathroom. I went to get up out of bed and slid onto the floor. For a few minutes, I tried getting myself up but was not successful. I started yelling for Eric. I was finally able to wake him up and tell him I was on the floor and could not get up. He came and got me up. He took me to the bathroom and then helped me back into bed. (At this time, we had no idea what had happened.) At seven o'clock in the morning, Eric got up and called our doctor. The doctor told Eric to take me to the hospital. Eric helped get me into the car. We lived only two miles from the hospital. They immediately admitted me and started running tests. By that evening, they informed us I had two strokes. I figured out one was probably at work and the other in bed. They had affected my motor skills on my left side, including my speech. Eric called my pastor's wife and asked for the prayer team to start praying. She was so concerned she drove in an ice storm to check on me. I was in the hospital for three days and sent home with Eric. The doctors and nurses were amazed at my progress.

I did have to go through physical therapy, occupational therapy, and speech therapy for several weeks. People are completely amazed when they look at me as I have little evidence of having had two strokes. I know it is because of the faith and prayers of many. God did this to his glory! I often tell people, "I am a walking, talking miracle."

What I have learned, I had shown the signs of a stroke, but we did not know what they were: (1) first the slurred speech on the phone, (2) my leg going out from under me, (3) falling out of bed and not being able to get up. Also, I learned there is power in the prayer of unity. In Matthew 18:19 (NIV), Jesus admonishes us, "Again, truly I tell you that if two of you on earth agree about anything they ask for, it will be done for them by my Father in heaven."

There were many miracles that happened that night. I did not fall down the steps. I drove myself home and got home safely. There were more miracles as the days passed. I was able to take a shower by myself just two days after the strokes. That stressful job provided short-term disability, so I was paid while I went through most of my therapy. They also provided medical insurance even for part-time employees. So they covered most of my bills. Because I was only part-time, I was also eligible for state insurance, which covered the rest of the bills, including therapy. I was also able to start a new job six weeks after being released from the hospital. God is so merciful and gracious!

Chapter 13

Ode to Joy

My relationship with Eric would never have happened had I not applied for financial aid after being told there was no more money and a scholarship not come through at the last minute. That fall school term was when Eric and I met. You never know what plans God has for you. Do not settle for anything other than God's will. We have been married for eight years. Eric is the most unselfish person I have ever met. He paid for my last two years of college so I could attend school full-time and complete my degree.

    I had no idea of the wonderful man God would bring into my life. I walked down the aisle on our wedding day to "Ode to Joy" instead of the wedding march. For God has truly turned my sorrow to joy.

    What I learned: (1) God is guiding my steps as I step out in faith; (2) God's plans are greater than we can imagine. I am reminded of Jeremiah 29:11 (NIV): "'For I know the plans I have for you,' declares the *Lord*, 'plans to prosper you and not to harm you, plans to give you hope and a future.'"

We had a small family wedding ceremony, with about thirty-five family members there. Because many family members were not able to show up until the day of the ceremony, we were not able to have a rehearsal; several things happened during the ceremony that brought many surprises and laughter to all.

Let me finish up by restating Romans 12:1 (NIV): "Take your everyday, ordinary life—your sleeping, eating, going to work, and walking around life—and place it before God as an offering." You will be amazed how God can take an ordinary life and make it extraordinary.

About the Author

Loretta has been a Christian for sixty years. As a child, she attended whatever church was within walking distance to their home.

As a teen, she was part of a Bible quiz team. They came in third place nationally. She memorized certain books of the Bible and competed against other youth groups in the organization.

Ten years after her father became a Christian, her parents became pastors; they pioneered churches. They went to small towns that either did not have a church, or the church had closed and reopened them. As an adult, she assisted in their first two churches, doing everything from helping to build an outhouse for one church to teaching Sunday school.

Loretta has always had a love for children. For twenty-five years, she taught first- and second-grade Sunday school in four different churches, two different denominations. She attended the weddings of many of her Sunday school kids.

She spent thirty-three years in a verbally, financially, emotionally abusive marriage that God brought her through and out of. After nine years of living alone and experiencing healing, God brought an amazing man who knows how to love her.

Her ministry is to encourage others. Her hope is that this book will do just that by using the word of God to bring hope and comfort to others.

CPSIA information can be obtained
at www.ICGtesting.com
Printed in the USA
BVHW021518140222
628969BV00021B/926